The Emotional Elevator and Taking Ownership

A guide to control and map the emotional mind

STUART A. HUNTER

Editor - Joshua Stuart

Balboa Press books may be ordered through booksellers or by contacting:

Balboa Press
A Division of Hay House
1663 Liberty Drive
Bloomington, IN 47403
www.balboapress.com.au
1 (877) 407-4847

Print information available on the last page.

ISBN: 978-1-5043-1816-7 (sc)
ISBN: 978-1-5043-1817-4 (e)

Balboa Press rev. date: 06/11/2019

For my M

And the biggest inspirations in my world, my two sons! They make me want to be better every day so I can be the best for them!

Introduction

Before we get on the "elevator" together, I'd like to let you know who you're getting on with. I am an ordinary guy sharing what I've found to be extraordinary. I try not to take myself too seriously (though, I kinda hope you do). I am not a psychologist, nor do I have a doctorate in human behaviours. I am sharing my lived expertise. Yes, I use scientific terms like the reptilian brain, the amygdala, the limbic system, and the prefrontal neocortex. As to why the brain does what it does, I am not going to get into all of that. There are more than enough books in the publishing universe about that for the scientifically minded. What I'll be giving you are relatable, simple metaphors that will give you a visual stimulus—something we have all experienced and used or encountered in our lives and ways in which we can use these visuals to change our emotional state and in turn be happier and lead a more fulfilling life.

Within the stories that I present in these pages, the emotional elevator is simply a metaphor, a visualisation that has, over the years, helped me deal with the consequences from situations that have arisen based on actions or choices I have made. I hope the emotional elevator will help you understand, change or combat situations in your life.

Taking ownership or responsibility is one of the biggest problems we face in society today. We are in a world where we pass the buck, so to speak. We absolve ourselves of any wrongdoing even though we have played an integral role in the outcome of our actions or reactions. This stunts our growth as a human being and stifles all of our relationships, whether it is in the workplace, between a child and parent, or with a spouse. The common denominator is me in every situation I face, and the common denominator in every situation you face is you.

I will share with you the principles related to taking ownership for my actions that I apply to my life. It is my hope that these principles help you prevent unhealthy patterns that can lead to the disintegration of your relationships.

I'll also be sharing inspirational quotes (I'm a big quote guy), but not like that annoying person on social media who posts a fluffy kitten picture with the words "smile and the world will smile back at you" ten times a day. I like relevant quotes, simple ones that remind us of our core values and a deeper connection to the concept of gratitude (why do the most miraculous things seem so mundane and why are we almost demanding more of everything?). We already have an overcomplicated life with our mobile devices and FOMO (fear of missing out) culture—let's slow it down and appreciate what we already have. My first quote is one that I keep on a board in my bedroom:

"I have learned that I still have a lot to learn."

- Maya Angelou

This phrase gives me comfort as I go through the ebbs and flows of life and closely ties in to the three major topics or themes of this book:

1) The Emotional Elevator—a metaphor for our emotional structure or state of mind.
2) The common denominator theory—in every situation in life, there is a common piece, player or person that helps perpetuate and create the ongoing situations we find ourselves in.
3) Taking Ownership—most fights, arguments, or disagreements etc can be resolved quickly and effectively when we take a step back and see the role we are playing.

I love helping people and I hope that when these three themes build upon one another, they'll help you look at your circumstances (or other people's) from a different angle and help you resolve some of the conflicts that are giving you stress in your life. In this fast paced world, *any* less stress has to be a good thing, right?

Don't think I have it all sorted out. Yes, I have bad days, and I don't always apply what I am writing about, but such is being human. Our brains are emotionally wired and sometimes we react automatically without thinking. Sometimes these knee-jerk reactions are good—fear helps keep us safe, but at other times our autopilot reactions can be detrimental to our wellbeing and to others around us.

One of the biggest realizations we all need to make is—drum roll please…

We are all hypocrites.

Being a hypocrite doesn't make you 'bad' either. It's not like we're all doing it on purpose, but if we can identify our occasional hypocrisy and take ownership, it will help resolve a whole series of events.

Pro Tip: this doesn't mean you get to be an arse and then just rebut with, "Oy. It's because I'm a hypocrite." Not cool at all.

Simply put, the hypocrisy I'm talking about is when we say something and do the complete opposite. Like, when you were a kid maybe your parents would yell or raise their voice at you to quieten you down. See what I mean there? Your parents weren't bad. They were frustrated, had a knee-jerk reaction and had a moment of hypocrisy and weren't aware of it.

Or for those without kids, what about the times you trade in your moral compass because "someone else is doing it?" You have a strong ethos in always arriving on time, but your best mate is always late. So, you decide you'll always be late for them because, "no biggie," they do it too.

No! This kind of passive aggressive hypocrisy is bound to cause problems in the relationship (yet we all do this to some degree or another).

The sooner we all realize the part we play in EVERY situation, the sooner we can begin to change and make things better.

"If you keep doing what you have always done, then you will always get the same result."

– Tony Robbins

Not rocket science, right? Yet how many of us fall into this exact same situation?

We always want things to change yet the majority of us look to others to blame, never turning that microscope onto ourselves. Time to start so we can get new results.

I have known many people that just seem to attract difficulty and chaos and who are always struggling with problems. You probably know or have met someone like this too. They ask your advice, yet they never ever take the advice you give and when you call them on it they might hang their head and say something like, "I know…" or "you don't understand."

This is the definition of an ASK HOLE—someone who asks for your advice but never takes it.

Don't be a giant ASK HOLE. If you want your life to change, you'll probably have to do something you've never done before.

I recently saw an example of youngish guy who happened to be experiencing the scientific definition of morbid obesity. He was clearly unhealthy and unhappy and wanted to make some changes in his life.

However, when he went to the supermarket, he refused to give up buying multiple packets of chips, lollies, and bottles of Coke.

I certainly don't judge the man for his choices (or maybe addictions), but there was something in his mind that couldn't separate his desire for change and the actions that he took to prevent that change from occurring. There was an element of hypocrisy in his life, and it's a hypocrisy that takes many different forms in our own lives.

How to Read this Book

As we move forward, all I ask is that you read with an open mind. Put aside your ego, which is an emotion that governs and makes decisions in your life more than you probably realize. Our ego often desires to be "right" and "look good" and has a constant thirst and hunger for "more." Be more than 100% honest with yourself and how you act and react to people and circumstances and know that maybe, just maybe, there could be a better or healthier way of dealing with things.

These are the questions I want you to remember

1. What emotional level am I on?
2. What part did I play?
3. Who or what is the common denominator?

Now, let's take a ride together up to Floor 1 on our Emotional Elevator.

Chapter 1

Your Mindset

"Mindset" is a series of beliefs or a belief structure.

Change your beliefs, change your mindset—change how you act and react.

So… what is the emotional elevator?

Another drum roll maestro…

It is a visual understanding—a mapping out of the emotional mind. It is the way our memories and emotions work and govern our behaviour.

Have you ever wondered why when you have a fight with someone you bring up all these past issues that have previously been dealt with? Some of those issues are years old, yet at the time this particular argument or disagreement their prevalence is paramount. How about when we are sad, and we remember all our past miseries? The loss of a pet, a sad movie, or an ended relationship can all trigger us, yet when we are happy and positive, nothing can stop us. We are like an express train full steam ahead, no stopping, not for anything or anyone! Jumping, bouncing off the walls with excitement and a lust for life. In those moments of joy and ecstasy we have no recollection of the feelings of loss or sadness or anger.

Ladies and gentlemen, welcome to the elevator theory!

So, let's map this out. Imagine a square, six-storey building with an elevator at one end. This building is similar to a hotel but without walls, hallways, or furniture. Each floor or level represents a different emotion. When the elevator door opens the whole floor is visible—every memory of that emotion is stored there and in some cases, depending on the severity and the depth of the emotional wound, it can still be as fresh as the day it happened.

Let's break down some of the basic definitions of our emotions. There are a great many facets to the complexities of our various emotions. Here I have generalized the main categories of what we feel and experience. All other emotions stem from these six:

Sadness
Anger
Happiness
Fear
Jealousy
Euphoria

Now, let's run some words associated with these individual emotions. Some, I am sure you will identify with.

Sadness: alone, blue, burdened, depressed, devastated, disappointed, discouraged, grief, gloomy, hopeless, let down, lonely, heartbroken, melancholy, neglected, pessimistic, remorseful, resentful, solemn, threatened.

Anger: aggravated, accused, bitter, cross, defensive, frustrated, furious, hostile, impatient, infuriated, insulted, jaded, offended, outraged, pestered, rebellious, revengeful, resistant, scorned, spiteful, testy, used, violated.

Happiness: adored, appreciated, cheerful, ecstatic, excited, grateful, glad, hopeful, jolly, jovial, joyful, loved, optimistic, pleased, satisfied, terrific, thankful, uplifted.

Fear: embarrassed, exposed, guilty, ignored, scared, frozen, mortality, rejection, failure.

Jealousy: abandonment, rejection, rivals, envy, humiliation, rage, obsession, revengeful.

Euphoria: elation, glee, excitement, exhilaration, animation, jubilation, exultation; ecstasy, bliss, rapture, rhapsody, intoxication, transportation, cloud-nine, heaven, paradise, utter happiness, joy, joyousness, delight.

Emotions truly govern our decision making, whether it be for good or sometimes for the worse. When we get angry and lash out, the outcome is generally less desirable. When we are struck with fear and we don't react there is a similar occurrence. When we are in love in the honeymoon period, we feel like we cannot do without that person and we need to make sometimes silly sacrifices to be with our new love. This can possibly lead to becoming unreliable or self-centred, or perhaps we risk losing jobs, friends, or careers.

Some of you are thinking *who, me?* Others may have a hand up with a guilty face (insert sad face emoji)!

There are also people who don't show any emotions at all. They keep a stoic face and on the outside seem calm and rational, yet when they have been pushed enough, they explode like an atomic bomb. Look out, because if and when this happens the fall out is massive and sometimes that loss of control is so extreme relationships end, or worse, people get physically harmed.

"Things (objects, circumstances) do not have meanings. We assign meaning to everything."

- Tony Robbins

Interesting fact, we know what pain is—we know we don't like or want it and we go out of our way (not?) to experience it. Though we all have experienced it, we cannot recall it or replicate it enough so that our body actually feels that physical pain or trauma without an external trigger (actual pain or trauma). We have all felt despair and fear, but when we are in our normal day-to-day life, we can't dial up the debilitating 'doubled over' fall, or the paranoia of wanting to hide in our house not showing our face to the world. Yet when we find ourselves in that fearful or scared state, we all of a sudden remember everything that ever scared us or perhaps even a time when someone made us feel belittled or when we felt ashamed. The same goes with anger. Those recollections of anger are not relevant to the issue at hand, but we bring it up and throw it around as a way to gain more weight behind our reasons for fighting with someone at the time. Sound familiar?

Euphoria is an interesting emotion—short lived and fleeting. There are not a lot of things we experience naturally that send us to this emotion hence the reason many turn to illicit drugs. It's the sort of free spirit, not-a-care-in-the-world whole body emotion we all love to feel. An otherworldly mind and body ecstasy! This is one tiny room that our emotional elevator brings us to because there are not a lot of times in our lives, we enter this room.

How many times have we felt that our partner is seeing someone else or is getting too much attention from someone else, or even showing too much interest in someone else?

We start doing irrational things, things we wouldn't normally do—checking our partner's phone, looking over their shoulder when they are texting, calling them on the phone when they are at work or at a work function if we know that other person will be there. We even lay there wide-eyed at night almost convincing ourselves because it is the way we believe it to be. Our jealous minds kick in and we feel sick or even become short tempered. We make snide comments to see whether or not they defend the other person and if they do…it's "aha, I knew it!" But really, we are probably being an arse and nasty and not fair to that other person. So of course, our partner will defend the other person, especially if they work with them. We created this mess of a situation and we set a trap for our partner to fail, just to help reaffirm that our theory is correct. We almost make it happen. The brain wants and almost desires a certain outcome, and we will do anything to achieve it.

What about that one person you just can't stand? They might seem to have it all going on and we are actually jealous of them. Your mindset is so hellbent on disliking them that everything they do annoys you. Your mind builds up dread seeing them but that person hasn't actually done anything wrong. They are living their life, just like you are living yours. If you analyze the root emotion of your driven hatred or jealousy, it will be closely related to admiration!

Yep, you want what they have. You admire that they have it, but you want it and because you don't have it, you transfer that emotion into jealousy or dislike.

The jealous mind is devious and cunning and can be an all-consuming, debilitating, and paranoid suspicious ruminating machine.

"What you fear the most will happen- that's the law."

- Shirley Hazzard

The less we sleep, the more irrational and out of control we become. It would appear that through our constant worrying, thoughts, or even our imagination, we ruminate and even create made up possibilities that may or may not ever eventuate. This causes our emotional elevator to speed up from one level of emotion to another, keeping us alert and in a state of anxiousness. We ALLOW this to happen! We then turn these ruminating thoughts into beliefs that we have created almost out of thin air, in turn keeping us awake and worse getting us upset, agitated, or even spiteful. In the end, we feel at a loss and in despair; all because our minds in this state are totally irrational! So, therefore, our circumstance makes no sense at all (and especially not to outsiders). Down the rabbit warren we go, spiralling downward, gaining speed and momentum. Deeper and faster we delve.

Have you ever had someone threaten you, maybe told you they were coming for you?

You become jumpy and begin to look over your shoulder. You lose sleep, almost too scared to go out because what if you run into that person? Or what if they are watching, waiting for the opportunity to get you?

Years ago, I received an email stating that a certain person was contracted to kill me and if I wanted to stay alive, I had to send £1500 to a specific bank account. Of course it was a scam but when I first read it my heart leapt into my throat. My heart quickened, my thoughts began moving at a million miles an hour wondering who could've been contracted to kill me, and what I had done to deserve this. In that very moment I knew it was a scam and yet my mind led me down that suspicious road and wasted so much mental time on 'what ifs.' The brain is an amazing worrying machine.

There are the actual physical stimuli that happen to our body as well—living in a perpetual state of fight or flight, draining the adrenals, constantly on edge. These along with lack of sleep, irrational thoughts, and fictitious scenarios will all most likely lead to an incredibly negative outcome. When the physical and mental combine they build up our fear and worry, making us snappy, short-tempered, and unpleasant.

It's incredible how we can worry so much sometimes, over nothing! Our own thoughts and imagination can create the most fantastical web of distraction and destruction.

Don't Believe Everything You're Thinking!

Chapter 2

Changing the Inner Script

Why do you think movies and TV shows are so popular? Why do so many people work 8-10 hours a day, get home pop the TV on and sit there for 3-4 hours then go to bed, get up, and repeat? What is it in our brains that makes us desire or need this? Some conspiracy theorists will say it is subliminal programming or it's there to keep us distracted from achieving more and becoming better—we are all sheep! Others will say it's simply harmless entertainment.

What about alcohol? What is the big attraction to drinking? There's 'just having a few to relax' and then there's the point of becoming drunk and out of control. Why do we need to loosen up all the time? Why do we need alcohol much like movies and TV, for an escape? Have we become a society that is miserable all day every day and need to escape our lives that badly? Isn't it time we did something to change this and enjoy our lives in a better, healthier, less destructive way?

Some people worry so much they can't sleep. Some are the dishonest type and in their work and they rip people off and work the system for their own benefit. These people are on edge all the time, highly strung, at risk of getting caught. Some of us resent other people for no real reason other than jealousy and when we take ownership (we will look further into this later on) we will see it has more to do with us than it has to do with them. Some of us hate our jobs yet we continue going there day after day, year after year, and each time a little piece of our soul dies with it.

* * *

There was this family I knew who lived in an incredibly nice area at a time when I didn't have a home and was just getting by. I thought they were super lucky, and I was a little envious of them. Then I found out that their nearly 20-year-old son was in a car accident, that left him severely brain damaged with half his body paralysed. Wow did I feel like an arse. How terrible for that family to experience and live with that trauma every day and here I was, envious of where they lived. Needless to say, it was a huge wake-up call for me. There is always another story that goes on behind closed doors and if we really knew we wouldn't want to trade our lives for anyone else's.

Things aren't always as they appear to be. We all wear masks and hide the ugly truth from people—another reason why social media is so popular. It reflects the life we want to have or the life we want everyone to think we are having. If everyone posted the ugly truth, how popular do you think it would be?

We have all experienced an emotional elevator scenario like the breakup from someone we thought was our true love, or even when sacked from a job. We get upset, cry, become destitute and stay at home, skip work, cry a river of tears and then we become angry, spiteful, resentful. Some never leave this emotion and go on to do some diabolical things all from rejection and an emotionally based reaction. It's the fear of "I can't live without them" or "I won't be able to function or find anyone that good again," "I am unemployable," or "I am no good, I suck." Then at some point we cycle through the positive and optimistic outlook—"It's for the best and I will find someone or something better," "Time for a new job anyway," "I wasn't really happy anyway." Sounds familiar, right?

Our brain is designed to survive! And we as humans are designed to survive. So why can't we tap into this when we are in the deepest of despair? Why do we have such a hard time reconciling our own humanity (we are flawed and perfect yet imperfect) while putting away our ego and reaching out for help if and when we need it? Why must we beat ourselves up, and cycle through all of these soul draining emotions?

Is it possible to shortcut this process? Damn straight it is!

Some people reading this and who knew me when I was younger will be scoffing at me here. Why? When I was 18-26 years old, I was an arrogant and emotionally out of control little shit. I had a temper and I'd fly off the handle at every little thing. With my upbringing I had a sense of entitlement and knew better than everyone!

Needless to say, I was in desperate need of change and education.

As I stand on my personal path I can turn around and look back to see how far I have come in my own journey.

If we are honest, all of us feel inadequate when someone we know has moved on or succeeded in achieving something good or amazing. When the green-eyed monster rears his ugly head, we use words like "gifted" and "lucky!"

Let's break down the word "luck" into an acronym and its true meaning:

L - labouring
U - under
C - correct
K - knowledge

When someone is lucky, it means he or she has worked their arse off in the right way, with the right amount of drive and perseverance and we should *should* look at this as an opportunity that we too can achieve similar things.

But to achieve something similar, you can't give up!

In my martial arts training studio, (the dojo), we have a sign on the wall:

A black belt is a white belt that never quit!

That's all it is about. Keep going and be persistent. Don't give up! If you hit a wall, scale it, dig under it, dig through it or work around it.

My *sensei* has a great saying, "build a bridge." In other words, "get over it."

We always have an opportunity to come to a complete stop, change our approach and ask the right questions from the right people.

if we have a healthy amount of emotional fortitude behind us, we too can succeed, as clichéd as it sounds.

Time for some honesty. Have you tried it—kept going, not accepting 'no' for an answer? Not letting a small obstacle stop you in your tracks?

If not, then how do you know? How is it easy for me to say when you haven't persevered past your first or second knockback? Sometimes there can be hundreds of knockbacks, but if you truly believe in something then preserve and don't give up.

This reminds me of the Colonel Sanders story.

He was retired and penniless and living out of his car. He believed that he had a special chicken recipe, which he took to various restaurants and chefs. He received 1,009 answers of no before he got one yes.

If he hadn't persevered, then there would be no KFC today (a world I don't want to live in!). He encountered 1,009 NOs!

How many of us would give up after 5, 10, 20?

I was a member of a group training fitness club. There was a lady there who had a prosthetic leg from the knee down. I was amazed at this lady's fortitude and determination and her ability to continue living life unaffected by her leg. She wasn't just getting by in the workouts either—she was smashing them, going hard, using the weights, jumping, and when it came to cycling, she would take the leg off and go hard one-legged! So again, a great lesson for me, when I hit the, "OMG I can't do anymore," wall and would see her out of the corner of my eye. I would tell myself that I had no excuse and to suck it up and keep going and go hard! Mind over matter, baby!

This is even more proof how our emotional mind really does govern our bodies on a daily basis.

Brain Space: Don't Rent it out Free of Charge

How many of us let a situation or scenario affect our whole day or even longer? Have you heard the expression when you hate someone it's allowing that person to live in your head rent-free?

Think about that—we are letting someone whom we dislike dominate our thoughts. The worst part is the person we dislike so intently has no clue that we are all bent out of shape over their actions. They are probably skipping through the day without a care in the world. Knowing this sometimes makes us even madder and makes us dwell and think about them even more. It's crazy. We need a stop button, a bin like we have on our computer—throw it in and empty it out!

When you look at it like that, it is actually quite ridiculous. Yet our beliefs are so strong from what WE tell our mind! Pause for a moment and think about that.

It's our thoughts and our emotional mind keeping that person or situation alive. Yes, they may have done the initial damage or caused a problem, but it is us, our thoughts that keep stoking the fire and keeping it a burning problem at the forefront of our mind, making it a much bigger issue than it needs to be.

Have you had someone cut you off in traffic on the way to work and narrowly avoided an accident? You beep your horn with great vigour as you push so hard on your steering wheel that you nearly set off the airbags. They casually lift the one hand wave, and yet that gesture leaves you even more infuriated with that stranger in the car. *They nearly caused an accident, how dare they?!* Your patience is now gone and you beep at every driver that does the slightest thing wrong, or even yell and abuse them. You get to work, shaking your head in disbelief all the way there. You probably glare at passers-by as if they were the driver and they're probably thinking, *sheesh, what's up with that guy?* The first person you see at work, you don't wait for them to finish asking how you are, you tell them what happened and not just what happened. You are super animated, with hand gestures and sound effects. The more people you tell the angrier and more agitated you become, and the story becomes bigger too! This early morning occurrence has now totally consumed you.

You carry this around all day, don't eat lunch, your work performance is below average, you are snappy and rude with your co-workers, and even when you get home you relay the story and get worked up into an agitated state again. You then decide that you need something to drink to take the edge off. An edge that YOUR emotional mind has created!

Let's slow this down. How can we put this situation and others involved into perspective? This kind of work in your daily life will take practice and time, so please be patient.

Thank goodness you had your wits about you and there was no accident. The driver of the other car might have swerved to miss another collision, there may have been a spider in the car, he might be new to the area and needed to get off at the next street—there are so many possibilities. But now you are starting to see and think rationally.

Without taking a moment to try and see the many possibilities, you take the driver's actions personally as if it were done on purpose to you. Then the day-long cycle of rumination and unhealthy emotions and thoughts begins.

Not only do you get to take yourself out of the rumination and unhealthy thoughts, you also get to CHOOSE to be thankful—thankful that you didn't have a crash and go through the whole domino effect of pulling over and stopping traffic, thankful you don't have to deal with other drivers being incensed and making themselves 'victims' while beeping you and yelling out their windows, thankful that you're not late for work, or thankful you don't have to be rushed off to hospital.

Consider how many times you have changed lanes or turned a corner and someone behind has beeped you. You have no idea why, so you raise one hand casually and wave like "thanks" or "sorry."

Or those times you have been walking to work and made eye contact with someone who looks like they're about to kill someone. In your head you thought *whoa, I'd hate to be their partner, or yikes—someone got up on the wrong side of cranky.*

The next time something like that happens, try not to let your emotions run away with you. Take a breath and take a step back mentally in order to see it from another angle. Give the other person the benefit of the doubt. We are often too quick to judge, to label, and all in too much of a rush to stereotype everyone and everything. Let's help this world calm down and take a touch of the aggression out. The aggression comes from our own emotional mind and our self-entitlement.

There are times we need to be strong, forthright and even aggressive, but not all of the time. Why do many of us find aggression to be the go-to emotion in so many situations? Is it how we are conditioned? Or is it because we don't know any better? Some individuals express aggression because it is the only emotion they know how to show. They've been conditioned through a traumatic home life or the neighbourhood they live in to show aggression as a means of survival. We don't need to allow someone to take their feelings out on us, but we also don't need to take their aggression personally. Often the way a person treats us is not a reflection of who we are as a person but what is going on inside the other person.

Chapter 3

Perceptions and Your Moral Compass

Our perceptions are based on a belief system we have been pre-programmed with (ideals we have learned from our parents), but often it is subconscious and so we must become aware of our perceptions, own them, and then learn to deal with them.

To expect others to see things exactly as we do is perhaps our biggest fault as human-beings. This pre-programmed belief system, for better or for worse, serves as our moral compass.

No two people can have the same moral compass, which is influenced by the sum total of the experiences we've had since infancy. It serves as the basis of our beliefs and how we react to certain things. Some of our actions and reactions (based on our belief system) are patterns replayed from watching how our parents responded and reacted in certain circumstances.

Our moral compass, when we're not aware of it, affects the emotional and reactive part of our mind, sometimes before we have the time to think about how to react in a healthier way.

Having children has been the biggest eye-opening experience of my life. It has been incredibly difficult and challenging at times. At times I have truly wondered what I was thinking taking on such a monumental task. However, fatherhood has been hugely rewarding. The number of emotions you can experience in ten minutes is almost beyond comprehension. Your sleep is hijacked and you are often pushed to the limit. Being a parent is a 24/7 job and it is exhausting.

BUT…

We can learn so much from children, such as their sense of innocence and the amazement and wonder that they have when they see something new, or something as simple as a butterfly.

There is also something about children that proves that we can change our circumstances while remaining persistent.

We were all children and for a period had no words or little cognitive awareness. When we were learning to walk, we would stand up and fall down. We must have done this hundreds of times and never did we slam our hands to the floor or throw our favourite fluffy teddy around in anger. Does a child even have the emotion or the feeling of humiliation?

The challenge and desire to walk is stronger than anything—it is all consuming. I have never heard of any infant that has tried and failed to walk several times only to throw their little pudgy hands in the air and say, "too hard" and never try again.

So, why as an adult or teenager do we come across slight resistance and then give up?

Where did this mindset come from—that it's okay to fail?

When we were infants, the thought of failure was not even an option. Nothing was going to stop us from walking. And yet our muscles weren't fully developed and our kneecaps not completely formed until age three. We hadn't even developed balance yet! It's incredible that we try or even persist at learning to walk. The infant's mind has such determination—a never give up attitude!

As an adult, we would say things like, *I have no kneecaps, I can't do it*, or *I tried like five times dude, just not possibl*e, or even *ouch, I hurt my butt—this is not worth the pain!*

Often, we let frustration take over and travel downward in our emotional elevator and get angry, some of us start hitting things, while others sit and stew in a quiet rage—all incredibly debilitating emotions. This anger and frustration cause us to use our emotional elevator to travel down even further to the basement floor of 'negative self-talk' telling ourselves that we're stupid, should never have tried, and that we're useless.

As we grow older it feels like we become jaded and cynicism kicks in. We second guess everything and we always think there is an angle or become disheartened by our experiences. Some of us become unimaginative, or are expecting to be let down or ripped off. All of this cynicism predetermines our reactions before we even allow the situation to unfold, but life doesn't have to be like this!

You can change what your thoughts are telling your mind, which will then change your beliefs. Change the elevator level your emotion is on and help change your focus.

Your emotional elevator will take you to a different level from your emotional brain. You can reach a level where your mindset flips to becoming empowered and determined. You start trying again and problem solving. Your self-talk even becomes more positive and you'll start telling yourself things like 'I knew I could do it,' 'I'm smart enough,' and 'I'm good enough.'

Try this exercise:

Next time you feel like you're failing at something and you sense that you're getting in the elevator to go to the basement floor (warning signs are destructive self-talk, the put-downs the negatives, the grunting, some form of self-harm, heavy sighing, hitting things, or verbal outbursts), take a moment. Stop. Take a breath. Walk away (for 5-10 minutes, not 5-10 years). Have a glass of water. Do some star jumps. Do anything you can to refocus. But work your arse off to not allow yourself to go down to the basement floor in your emotional elevator. Tell yourself, 'I can do this.' You can change and choose which floor you're on and use the elevator to get out of your funk!

The more you are able to control that elevator, the quicker you can resolve and move on—and you'll have a whole lot less stress in your life.

* * *

What is it that we don't want to show in front of our friends and peers? Humiliation? Failure? Is it that you don't want to be laughed at? Do you want to project an aura of perfection?

The best way to learn is to make mistakes. To fall flat on your face builds character. What fun would life be if everything were easy and everything we ever attempted we did perfectly? Where's the challenge?

Where's the resilience (you must cultivate it)?

Where's the mind power of overcoming obstacles (we must cultivate the mind)?

Where's the self-esteem boost from failing so many times that it stretches us and makes us dig deep until we finally achieve our goal?

Use these experiences as a mindset for positive growth, not a negative put-down.

We would never reach our emotional state of euphoria if we never gave ourselves the opportunity to fail and fall. We succeed from our own hard work, our sweat and tears and our determination. The reward is all yours if only you can feel it, sense it, appreciate it.

The outside noise you sometimes hear from peers and strangers is just a mask to cover up their own insecurities and the hope that they don't fall flat on their face. That noise has nothing to do with you.

Can you see how over time we have taught ourselves to quit or not even attempt new things? The perceived mountain of problems we often 'foresee' is all in our emotional mind; not a mountain at all and nothing like the actual task in front of us.

Instead of focusing on the "mountain," try to focus on the single step in front of you. You'll be able to see any potholes (challenges) that arise and you can avoid them, all the while making it up that 'mountain' much quicker "if you made it your singular focus. Then take a moment to stop and look back to see how far you have actually travelled. You may be amazed at how far you have actually travelled. Give yourself a pat on the back and forge forward!

Chapter 4

Eliminating or Reducing Anger and Worry

"The same hammer that shatters glass forges steel."

- Anon

In regard to pesky inanimate objects:

How can an inanimate object have an evil conscience and go out of its way to upset you or be 'deliberately difficult?'

Sounds kind of silly when I say it like that, eh?

This is what I do, and it may be bordering on madness, but when I come across an inanimate object that just isn't complying, instead of getting angry I get in my elevator and go to my happy level. I begin to tell myself how silly it is that I am being beaten by a piece of plastic or a hammer and nail or a bolt and start to laugh (not a crazed laugh—a fun laugh). I create a humorous environment to stop me from travelling down to the basement level of frustration and anger and I inject fun into it. Is this always easy to do? Hell no! But what helps is if I look at my parameters. If I am on a time restraint, I'll tackle the task when I have more time. Or I'll check if I'm placing unrealistic expectations on myself. The hardest question to ask is *do I need help with this?*

Many of us have experienced something similar to this. Next time you come across a situation that doesn't run smoothly or work out in your favour, stop yourself from going down to the basement level in your emotional elevator. We are all creatures of habit, some of these habits are healthy and some aren't. We can change our habits by changing the way we go about tackling situations, which will then lead to a different outcome or less day to day stress.

Our biggest enemy is our self-talk, and this phrase is one of the worst: "I don't have time for this!"

We create time restraints, which then create frustration, anger and disappointment, and down we travel in our elevator. Why do WE place time restraints on things? Who said it has to be done by a certain time or it should take a certain amount of time?

It is these unrealistic expectations and these thoughts that cause this pressure and tension.

We should tackle our task in however long it takes because it needs to be done right first time.

Again, your mindset and your thoughts create most of your tension, anxiety, and overall stress.

If you are already agitated or have "I don't have time for this" on your mind when trying to resolve a problem, you have already stacked the outcome against the other person. They have no hope! Even though you desire peace and harmony, you expect resistance and aggression from the other person and that is exactly what you get.

If you work to remove the emotion from the situation and can drop the ego and pride, you'll see the other person's point of view as well. And when you can work from that place, you almost always bring a calmer demeanour and are more likely to achieve a better outcome.

If you want a different outcome, then you need to change your approach!

Take ownership—no one else is to blame but you!

The way you address a situation or person will determine your outcome!

Honesty time!

Are you getting the results you desire with less stress?

How is your approach to current circumstances working for you?

What works and what doesn't? Can you see a pattern?

Control where you allow your emotional mind to travel to in order to help and handle the situation in a healthier way.

You can't control others, even though you may try, but you can control yourself, only if you choose to. It will take work, but you need to rewire and redirect your automated responses.

Out of the Mouth of Babes

Something my son said when he was only 6 years old was simple yet profound, and so straight to the point it nearly made me have a car accident from choking up with emotion and awe (proud dad moment).

His insight proved to me that though adults think we have it sorted, there is so much we can learn from children.

I have applied this insightful saying to my everyday life: "out of the mouth of babes."

So, what did my son say? (Hang on—I'm getting there!)

He had done something careless that hurt his brother. I went on to tell him he needed to learn to respect and look out for his brother. I asked him if he understood.

"Yes," he replied. "I get it. Can we move on now daddy?"

But I kept asking him and he finally blurted out:

"Daddy, the less you think about it, the less you will worry about it."

Take a moment to really think about that.

The less we keep the situation alive in our mind ruminating on the problem, the less we will worry and lose valuable time on it.

Just like the near car accident and allowing that situation to spoil the rest of your day.

Do this simple exercise:

Next time you are sad or upset, think about all the things that make you happy. Get up and become active or take a walk outside. This will help you get off the sad floor in your brain and get in that emotional elevator and start rising to happier and healthier levels.

Motion changes emotion.

Don't believe everything you're thinking

There are millions of examples of how our emotional minds govern and rule our lives.

Emails and text messages can be the devil. Something can be so blunt that we get offended, or the content could be super innocent and yet the emotion we assign to it while reading the text can change everything!

How much time is spent with text messages or emails, back and forth, trying to explain what the last text meant because the recipient read into that text with their own emotion? If we are feeling frustrated, we will read a simple text with disdain or add an emotion that just isn't there. It all depends on which floor we let the emotional elevator take us to.

Emails and texting are a valuable means of communication, but not always desirable when trying to express something with emotion. It can be incredibly misleading and often we can put something in a text or email we can't quite say to another person's face.

The miscommunication can get frustrating, and we are inching closer to our graves by creating so much tension that our pulse rate, heart, and head feel like they're about to explode—all over what started out as a simple text message that probably should have been said face to face and resolved in a fraction of the time.

Why is face to face better? Because we can see and hear the emotions. We can look into the eyes of that person and read their body language.

Often when we're emotional, we let texts and emails run off before the brain can filter. When you feel that frustration and anger and aggression, maybe hit pause and ask yourself, *"Is it wise to send? Have I lost control? Are my emotions running away with themselves?"*

Once you have typed and sent the words, they can never be unseen. Wait, let it sit, sleep on it. What emotional level are you on? Can you or do you want to change it?

If you need to address something emotionally charged or of great concern to you, it is far better to ring up or meet in person. Do not send your thoughts via email or text. It is going to be time consuming and super ineffective. Remember that you want less stress!

Not everything goes according to your plan.

What often happens when we go through a difficult situation is we begin problem solving based on our moral compass. We think about the actions we can take and try to plan out what our desired outcome would be. If we do everything a specific way it will all work out great. We present this solution to our friend in need of a confidante and we are proud we have solved the problem.

The problem is not the problem, it actually lies within the variables of the "solution", whatever it may be. But we don't know this and those variables on the way to our "solution" increase when more people are involved. Then when it doesn't go according to our plan, we get upset. Our pride is hurt, we become angry, and we might even sabotage the rest of the outcome because our anger has consumed us. Our defensive walls go up and are easy to raise but take a long time to take down. All because things didn't go according to OUR plan. We become incensed that the person or people haven't appreciated our attempts to resolve the situation.

When you look at it objectively this kind of thinking doesn't serve anybody.

How is this kind of thinking helping?

Is this about our ego?

Is it our moral compass and pride and desire to be the Mr. Fix It superhero that is preventing us from looking at things objectively and effectively solving or helping to reach a resolution? Whatever happened to simply being good just to be good?

How can we be sure that our way is the ONLY way to solve any given problem?

Or is that we are in the midst of an altercation and our emotions are already heightened and nerve endings have started to fray? Our recall reaction kicks in before we know what is happening and we travel in our elevator to that level of rejection and it is all amplified and becomes blown out of proportion.

Can we control this?

Of course, it's an emotional response. When we are enlightened and aware, we can stop the knee-jerk reactions and create new synapses in our brain and reroute them, so we are less inclined to keep replaying the emotional mistake we always seem to make.

Chapter 5

Taking Ownership

If someone brings up a problem they have with you,—maybe it's the way you act, or you have done something to annoy them—hopefully it is brought up in a calm, civil manner. "Hey, there's something I need to discuss with you." If it isn't, here is where we can dial it back and create an even calmer setting to resolve the situation.

For starters if the TV is on then turn it off, not just on mute because we will constantly look back to the TV the whole conversation (and not because we are rude or bad).

Ed Vul, an associate professor of psychology at the University of California, San Diego studies intelligence and behaviour with a focus on how we process information. Summarizing Vul's work, basically we'll keep looking back at the TV and not our conversation partner because our eyes will always be drawn to the most powerful visual cues in any given setting. So, to give our full attention it's best to hit the off button.

There two main benefits of doing this:

1. Your partner or person addressing the issues feels 100% heard and validated (super important).
2. You are actually giving your attention to listening, not dividing it. It's a win-win!

Instead of having your defensive walls automatically shoot up 10 miles high, listen to what the other person is actually saying. Stop the elevator and remove the emotion and look at the situation from their perspective. One more time: *their perspective.*

They are a human being with their own feelings and their own moral compass.

Don't dismiss or justify. Listen and take ownership for the part you have played in them feeling the way they do. Apologize for making them feel that way. Begin to discuss a solution—what do they need? Help them to feel validated and that they are important in your life. If you truly care about this person then you will adapt to make things more harmonious. Do not give them lip service or say what you think they want to hear just to hurry up and end the awkward conversation. You're avoiding and evading and in the end, it will just amount to further issues.

It's irrelevant if you agree with them or not (you're taking ownership). The fact is, they feel the way they feel. Most people wouldn't bring up issues unless they didn't feel strongly about them in the first place.

Also keep in mind this person may have been ruminating on bringing this up with you for days, weeks, or even months, so there is a lot of thought behind this. They could be all tied up in knots or have lost sleep over it all. So, give them the due time required to help them resolve this.

Why is it that when we get in our elevator we cross our arms, our pride puffs our chest out and we are mortified that someone could be unhappy with us? In some way we're thinking *this is a preposterous silly allegation I'm being charged with and it is not worth making a fuss over.* But that's YOUR brain and YOU wouldn't react that way! But it's not about YOU. Our arrogance and ego get in the way. The brain literally stops receiving information, as if we're under attack so bunker down, put on that bullet proof vest, and fight back. Dramatic much?

If you are honest with yourself right now, you will acknowledge that you have been in this circumstance before. And quite possibly at fault!

When your partner, friend, or boss is addressing an issue with you, this is not the time to make it open slather. If you have a grievance with this person, now is not the time to address it. It will be seen as an aggressive retaliation and a sign of immaturity.

Of course, you are also justified to have an issue with the way that person made you feel at some point, but choose wisely when to speak up about it.

Tit for tat never produces a good end result—if anything it amplifies it all and the original issue gets lost and never resolved.

I have been in a situation where I brought up something and the other person just threw stuff back in my face. Realising what was happening I calmly said, "I do want to address that issue, but can we address this concern I have brought up first? This is the first time I'm hearing about your concern and I would love to sit down at a separate time to address it. But now is not the time." This approach worked incredibly well (though I must admit it took a bit of self-control not to allow my emotional elevator to travel to the angry level).

To sum it all up, we need to be careful that when someone brings up a grievance with us that we don't treat that as an open playing field to air all of their dirty laundry at once.

The Physical Manifestations

It always amazes me how our mind and emotions govern our bodies and affect us physically.

When we worry about something, we can get stomach cramps, diarrhea, or even loss of appetite. When we become nervous we get what we call 'butterflies' in your stomach. Let's ponder that for a moment—*the brain generates thoughts strong enough to affect us physically in our stomach and bowels.* How does that make any logical sense (yes, you can Google it and I can list the science behind it, but I am making a separate point about the wonder of it all)? It is a chain reaction, brain to body, that can be strong enough to cause us to double over. All of our thoughts and emotions—super powerful stuff.

Our brains are powerful spiritual machines, even if we can't move objects with our mind or read other people's thoughts (thank god for that—WAY too much to handle!).

The Chinese believe in the *dantian* (energy centre). Some Indian cultures believe in the *prana* (life force). Australians call it their gut or gut feeling.

The Japanese believe the soul lives in the *hara* (sea of energy), which is located at the navel, about two inches inwards from the skin.

It cannot be a coincidence that this is the same area of the body that becomes affected when the brain and our thoughts and emotions run rampant.

The Japanese ancient custom Seppuku, also known as hari-kari was predominantly used by Samurai as a way of cutting the soul out of one's body, to avoid falling into enemy hands and to avoid shame and also possible torture. There is the reported case of **Minamoto no Yorimasa** in the battle of Uji In 1180. It seems more than a coincidence to me that this the area of the body they chose to 'cut out'.

We can get so worried and worked up it actually makes us sick and run down, with no motivation or desire to do anything. If you look up the definition of depression, it means feelings of severe despondency and dejection.

Notice it starts with the word feelings? If you look up the definition of feelings the second definition is an idea or belief, especially a vague or irrational one.

Where do our beliefs come from? Everything we experience from being a baby, through to our school and our working career and also our genetic imprint from our parents. There is also our own moral compass and individuality all smooshed together that makes us US.

What fuels our desires?

What is it that makes us want a certain type of car, whereas our friends desire another? What about our fashion sense, or any other decision made on beliefs or preferences? It stems from our ego, which has an underlying need to feel safe and to feel understood—yet most of us lack the understanding of the underlying context of the 'wants' of the ego. Simply put, if we don't understand what our ego wants, then it comes out as 'look at me mummy and daddy,' 'I need to get a good score on my exams (to best a sibling, to get attention, to feel the safety that it will help you do well in life, to feel like it will make you look attractive or valuable in another's eyes), or even 'I want a promotion at work.'

When we fail or don't succeed, where does it hit us the most? Our life force centres—our stomachs! So many thoughts and desires all concentrated in one area of the body.

It would be easier if our little finger just started to ache a bit, but no, it is a powerful reaction straight to our core that can double us over.

All from what? The ego living inside our brain.

Truly mind blowing!

Taking ownership in the workforce

Taking ownership is something people don't do enough of in this day and age, especially in the workplace.

I remember when I was a child going in to buy some shoes with my parents. The shop assistant would measure the length and width of my feet, go and get the shoes for me, help me try them on, ask if they were comfortable and ask me to walk up and back a few times to make sure the heel didn't slip.

As an adult, I walk into the shop and tell the assistant my size and put them on, and the only other question is, "Will that be all for today?" There seems to be a lack of care in customer service. "Not my job," or "I don't get paid enough," seem to be the permeating attitudes.

The way it appeared in my dad's era of work was that you work yourself to the bone for one company until you get a gold watch, a handshake and then retire. Now that seems null and void. People don't stay in their jobs for a long time anymore—it is all about what more can I get, or I am not being treated properly.

I went into a phone store to upgrade my device and the sales girl was distracted by her own phone. Her football team was playing that day and in the time I was there she was constantly checking the score!

Have we become that entitled that our job is seen as getting in the way of our leisure activities?

I was in a grocery store on a Sunday night with a full trolley. There were two staff members chatting with each other, but none of the checkouts were open. One staff member looked at me and said, "You can use the self-serve."

After a little sarcastic (but kind on my part) back-and-forth, one of them opened a checkout lane.

Both examples, the sales girl at the phone store and the staff at the grocery story show a reasonable customer being treated in an unreasonable manner and employees not taking ownership. If an employee is hired to do a job—whether it be pumping petrol, sweeping floors, or a member of Parliament—they need to take ownership, which means they do it to the best of their ability. When did half-arse become the standard?

A good friend of mine is an instructor where I practice karate. One day we were talking about the club membership numbers dropping. At the time there was a lot of competition with new martial art training centres opening up in the surrounding areas and it seemed people weren't knocking down the doors to learn martial arts as much. As we spoke, he said the most remarkable thing to me. He said he thought maybe it was his method of teaching that was causing the drop in numbers.

He didn't blame the marketing department, or the managers, or the economic climate, or the other clubs opening up around the corner. No, he turned that microscope around to himself and started questioning whether he was a contributing factor, and what he could do change and improve.

How many of us do this?

When we are faced with a situation is it always someone else's fault. Are we that blame free and perfect that we haven't contributed an ounce?

Any job or relationship or situation you are in, YOU are a contributing factor. How you act, react, your tone, your performance all affect the interaction. Sometimes it's not you at all, but most times it is—after all, you are the common denominator in each situation.

Question time:

How many of us put our hands up when we have messed up regardless of the consequences?

Why do we think that coming up with excuses is better than putting up our hand and admitting we had made a mistake?

How much easier and more time efficient would it be to sort out a problem if we admitted it and took ownership instead of creating excuses and going the long way just to reach the end conclusion that we made a mistake?

My favourite saying is a Japanese proverb— "Nana korobi ya oki."

Fall down seven times, get up eight.

It's about resilience and not giving up—being stronger than yesterday!

It's Only Temporary

When we are going through a tough time, we often feel like it's so heavy or there's no way out, yet six months or a year after it is all resolved it really has no emotional effect on you. Yes, the circumstances you may be in may have changed—different house, split from a partner—but you don't have the same emotional attachment or that downtrodden feeling like you can't go on. You get on with your life. Sure, it will sting sometimes, but you are stronger for it. Like I mentioned earlier, it is not so easy to simply change our state and stop the automatic sequence of our emotional elevator that is ingrained in us from an early age. It's not easy to change our moral compass either.

That compass has guided us, led us, and set us on a path for a long time and it's hard (but possible) to recalibrate.

You can smile or laugh again, and maybe you are even sleeping better. So, the saying, "it's only temporary," is so spot on.

How annoying is it when you are in that horrid situation and you have that one friend who says, "The grass is always greener," (we will look at my take on this saying later on), or "Chin up bud," or "It'll pass."

Although these are words of wisdom, they are not what you want to hear at the time.

If you are honest you don't really know what you want to hear, even when a solution is placed before you. What you actually want is to be heard and understood, and given the space to figure it out yourself (with some help).

The one who falls and get up is so much stronger than the one who never fell!

Here's something we are all guilty of—from a single thought you can make your own world like a real life *Days of our Lives* soap opera. It can start with a simple, "I wonder…," or "Why haven't they replied," "Have I done something wrong," or "Why didn't they say hi to me?" We then create unreal scenarios out of thin air, thoughts spinning out of control like a Danish pastry, layer upon layer of emotions and feelings. We even go as far as avoiding our friend or assuming what we think they will say and what we would do and then reply to them in our head and the problem becomes worse and worse. We create emotionally charged fictitious arguments, all from our imagination, which causes us a massive amount of anxiousness and worry—for a scenario that never even happened!

Then when you finally meet up and talk, you discover that there wasn't a single ounce of truth to what you were imagining. Days, weeks, and months of worry all for nothing. We know this is unhealthy and yet we do it over and over again. We get in our little elevator and head down to the level where we create fictitious scenarios that cause us stress and pain. Some of our elevators are broken and grounded on that level for a long time, so much so that we don't even know which way is up.

There is power in a single thought and we must harness our thoughts, so we avoid the basement level in our emotional elevator.

We need to "Nana korobi ya oki." Fall down seven times, get up eight.

Easier said than done. I've been there. At one point in my life it took every ounce of my being to claw my way back and I nearly didn't make it out alive. It was so bad I was on anti-depressants and that was only so I could go through the motions of simply functioning. Every day I did what I had to, would sleep and then oversleep and would put my mask on to pretend like all was good. But underneath I was screaming. I wanted to collapse, and no one knew what was going on except those really close to me.

Some of us do this perfectly—walk around smiling while crying out for something different underneath, getting on with what has to be done, and doing our best to keep the demons in our head at bay. For some people (not everyone) the ruminating thoughts and emotions keep you stuck in your elevator on the floor of despair.

One of my partners could never understand how I was able to be sick, throwing up in the toilet one minute, and the very next all smiles and back to work teaching as if nothing was wrong. This is an example of how the mind, our thoughts, and our emotions are so powerful, and we have the power to control (or at least better manage) our physicality.

At one point in my life I experienced a form of depression, and I can put my hand up and say that I contributed to the circumstances (I take ownership for my part) that led to my depressive episode. But it didn't mean I was in control of what happened—you can't control what other people do and say. They have their agenda and their reasons and their perceptions, not facts. They have their own moral compass. There are many perceptions in a situation which are based on one's own belief system and their moral compass. You CANNOT expect anyone to understand how you feel. They can maybe empathize, but not understand. Expecting them to understand and feel the gravity of maybe what they've done to you (according to your perception) is only leading you down the elevator to frustration.

Let me share part of my experience with you. I went in on a business venture with a family member. I was so excited to be moving forward in this venture because of the experiences I was obtaining and the difference I was making. Most of all it involved one of my passions—the stuff that dreams are made of.

I was on cloud nine. I would ask the right questions and I would do my utmost to do my part in the business. Unbeknownst to me, it was all a sham—dishonesty and smoke screens and a web of deception.

When I uncovered the truth, it sent me reeling and then when it came for the other partner to step up and be accountable—it never happened. More lies, more deception, and for someone like me who gives 120%, it was absolute devastation.

In a single day my world came crashing down.

I literally felt my whole being, including my brain, had just shut down. I was tired, yet an insomniac. My brain was asking "how?" and "why?" nearly non-stop. It could not comprehend what had happened. It was trying to search for justifications and rationalizations, but the person I was up against had been doing this a long time, and I was no match for them. The problem with people not taking ownership is they leave other people distraught and confused—especially when they are in denial of their part and they can't or won't be honest and take any ownership. I sometimes wonder how people can sleep at night.

I started resenting myself for being Mr Positive and thinking good thoughts and that good will come. I started quoting negative things like, "nice guys finish last," and "you can't please everyone." The funny thing was, I could identify what was happening to me but at the early stages I was unable to combat and correct it. My elevator was grounded; no power, stuck in the level of depression and despair. All my training in martial arts, all my breaking through barriers achieving and pushing past the comfort zones had all halted. The term being "broken" was true, at least during that period of time.

As it turns out, good has come out of that experience. Without it I most likely would not be writing these pages, and I'd be still in my situation where I was unhappy. Ultimately, I needed to be the best father for my children and that has been my driving force. I understand that I had a part in my temporary demise and I have stepped back, owned it, and reassessed my situation. My boys are my driving force, so I feel I have done what is best for them as well as for me.

None of us are perfect. We all falter and make mistakes. How else are we to learn?

People resist taking ownership in different ways

My favourite is when you want someone to take responsibility for his or her actions. You ask a question like, "why did you do this?" or let them know, "this isn't acceptable," and it's like they immaturely stick their fingers in their ears while singing, "I can't hear you." It could be in a text where they ignore or answer all the other questions yet omit the area where they're at fault or the part where they need to explain their actions. It's frustrating and unnecessary. How much easier would it be to have problems resolved in the shortest amount of time possible? Do you see how you can really prolong a seemingly quick situation with an honest answer by taking ownership for your part?

Now here's the downside if you are a habitual avoider.

At the time you think you have outwitted the person. You assume you are either smarter than the other person, or have avoided a confrontation. Maybe your ego is really that big that you tell yourself that you do no wrong or it's easier to label them in your mind as a "problem" person.

Do you feel that you have a barrage of people so intent on asking question after question that the problems just don't seem to go away? This is probably because you have set a precedent by being "the avoider."

Each incident intensifies and compounds because the person has already prepared for your abstinence and continual arrogance by avoiding responsibility. IF you had taken ownership and answered the questions in the past by being honest and seeing your part in the problem, then the months or years of continual questioning would probably not be there.

Yet our ego's self-importance gets in the way and we think we know better, or have outwitted the other person. Maybe you feel you have it all figured out. Alarm bells always ring for me when people say, "I don't need to learn anymore, I am right!"

The only thing you have really achieved is depriving yourself of time and beauty in your life. You have cost yourself a heap of time instead of living and enjoying the fruits of your hard work and laughing and enjoying what you have. We spend all those hours at work so we can enjoy our lives, hobbies, friends, or kids. But we seem to want to tie all that up with stress and problems. We think we know better and try to avoid the real issues. Yes, they are uncomfortable, and yes, they will make you humble and have to apologize—but that is where the real personal growth lies! It's exciting!

The challenge is to truly become aware of how we affect others and the changes that need to be made.

Try this:

If you are an avoider or even if you're not, next time some asks you to be answerable for something and you think "I haven't got time," think about this—have you got time for the amount of back and forth texts or phone calls?

When you take ownership and then they continue at you, you then have the grounds to say, "I have answered honestly, gotten to the facts, and have taken ownership. I have no more to say. Now it's your turn to accept it and move on."

I happen to be the type of person that if I don't get the answer I am after I will ask it in multiple ways from different angles, and not let up. I have been told I am like a dog with a bone! My emotions and thoughts become suspicious. *What are they hiding? Why can't they answer?* This is of course because of my own moral compass settings, due to my life experiences.

Have we become a society where telling a lie is better than honesty? What is it that we fear? Is it not being liked? Or is it not wanting to upset the other person?

Time and time again we learn the hard way. As much as honesty can initially sting, the sting is temporary and we can resolve issues and move on without dragging things out. Maybe we can even earn some respect from the other person by being humble, honest and taking ownership.

Next time you are having an argument, put the emotional elevator on hold. Don't get it in and let it descend. Hold back your automated defense system that often kicks in (because if you want a better outcome, you need to approach the situation differently). Truly listen to the other person, put what you think aside and take your emotions out of the equation. Think about their point of view and then give them the honest truth. See if it leaves fewer stones unturned. Monitor if it takes less time to resolve. Pay attention to whether or not the outcome is far better.

If we constantly lie or try to cover our tracks, we are actually teaching that person that we are shifty and dishonest!

Ownership time—have we given this person the truth or have we tried to weasel out of things?

Chapter 6

Trusting Your Gut

I have been extremely fortunate to meet a variety of people throughout my life, some who have made a tremendous impact.

One such man was proficient in Karate and helped me a great deal with my techniques by giving me little things to work on to improve my skills.

He was a great sounding board and had quite a wealth of knowledge. One day as we were chatting, he imparted to me such an insightful passage of words that it changed me.

"Some people come into your life for a reason, some a season, and some a lifetime. However long it was, be thankful for the gifts you received from them."

- Anon

It may not have the same resonance and profound effect on you, but at the time I was struggling. I had taken a big hit and was reeling from it. My mask was only working so well and this guy seemed to see right through it.

Later in that conversation I tried to brush him off after he asked me if I was okay.

He looked directly into my eyes, and his gaze pierced through my mask to my soul.

"Your soul knows what it needs to do, but your mind is fighting it," he said.

At that moment it was like time stopped, a small vortex opened up, and everything was silent. I felt like I had been punched in the stomach.

My soul cried out with "what am I supposed to do now?" and then there was a feeling of joy, because I was finally having a breakthrough.

It was a mix of comfort and despair, my emotional elevator was going haywire—elation, fear, anxiousness, satisfaction and so many other emotions all in a split second. After he left, I actually burst into tears—a soulful cry of relief.

This haunted me for days and I tried to deny what my soul was telling me, my mind in defensive mode. But finally, my soul won.

From that day forward I always listen to what my soul is telling me, and I can assure you it has not led me astray.

Trust your soul, your intuition, your gut. Turn off the mind and listen to what your soul is crying out for.

Right or wrong?

We are always too scared to make the wrong decision. We want to make the "right" choice and know with 100% certainty that we are making the right decision to fix our problem. The perfect decision! The failsafe. The "I have done no wrong" mindset. This is such a strong part of our mental psyche. But can you can see how this is an impossible scenario to expect?

We always look at it this way: what's the right thing to do and what's the wrong thing to do?

We are so conditioned to right and wrongs!

I am not talking about going out and harming other people, or yourself. I am merely talking about whether to move to a new house, or break up with someone, or change jobs!

There is neither right nor wrong.

You're scratching your head, right?

Whichever you choose, you will make it work. Your resilience as a person will make it work. The DNA of human survival will make it work. The sun will still rise every day. So, what are you afraid of—a choice that was deemed wrong? Is that coming from your moral compass or someone else's?

Do you know anyone who seems to have so much thrown at them, yet they seem to cruise through life without it affecting them in the slightest?

Are they arrogant, or do they just keeping moving forward wearing their mask? Without a doubt.

Is it possible for us to pick up and keep going? Of course, it is. We always have.

Instead of looking at the worst outcome possible, change your mindset, reprogram that moral compass. It won't be easy, but it is totally doable.

How?

It seems we are programmed to always look at the worst-case scenario. This can be a good thing if we only allow our emotional elevator to stay there for a short time. It can be a source of motivation, a way for us to look at the doom and gloom and resist and hop in our elevator and change levels. We can make it our driving force to make sure that outcome never happens!

But some of us stay there and we feel all hope is lost and we give up!

What can be accomplished by worrying at 3 am?

Not much, so turn the brain off. Easier said than done, right?

Try meditating. Focus on your breathing—counting one as you breathe in and two when you exhale, counting all the way up to ten and then start again. Each time you'll focus on breathing deeper and deeper, taking slower and longer breaths to fill your lungs so much that your stomach should rise up and deflate as you breathe in and out.

This takes practice. It is natural for the mind to wander and start thinking. It is not used to being silenced. But it's okay to simply bring your thoughts back to your body and your breathing.

Focus on feeling your pulse through your heart. Then try and focus on it by trying to feel your pulse through your kidneys and then other parts of your body: hands, feet, legs, and so on. Don't let your brain say this is too hard. Focus! The more you do it the better you will become at silencing the mind, and you will be able to be silent and still for longer!

This is the best thing for your mind, body and spirit! This dates back thousands of years with *Qigong*.

Try this—put the book down here and set a timer on your phone for five minutes.

Sit cross-legged with your hands resting gently on your knees or lie down placing your hands on your stomach and breathe deeply. Try not to fall asleep.

Silence your mind and let it rest!

Chapter 7

I'll Finally Be Happy When... (Hint: No, You Won't)

The grass is always greener

Are you familiar with this expression?

Here is my take on it.

Your neighbour has an immaculate backyard; lush, thick green grass, beautifully maintained pathways, a gazebo, a crystal blue swimming pool—even the garden shed tucked in the corner is clean and tidy.

You think to yourself, "the grass is greener over there." You buy the house from your neighbour because your "need" for this amazing backyard has consumed you. You believe that once you obtain this, your ego will be satisfied, and you will want for no more. You will have everything your heart desires. You could invite your friends over and they would be super impressed.

You move into the house on a lovely summer day, and you are loving life while spending time in your new yard! While taking a dip in the pool, a great satisfaction resonates throughout your body and mind. You are "happy."

A few weeks pass by and the pool starts to turn green. The paths begin to grow weeds. The shed is chaos and after a month the grass is patchy and dying.

You stand with your hands on your hips scanning the backyard, shaking your head, and asking what happened. "Where did my 'happy' go?"

You look over the fence to your old backyard. It is green with thick, lush garden beds. The pathways are well-manicured. You think, *wow my old yard wasn't that bad after all.*

What happened?

You are what happened.

You put the same preparation and maintenance into your new backyard that you did to your old backyard—little to none.

The previous owner most likely spent time attending to their garden every weekend while you were too busy doing other things. The new owners of your old house have invested time in fixing up the mess you left behind.

The grass may be greener on the other side, but instead of coveting and being envious, maybe look at what you can do to obtain a similar result in your own yard first.

Invest the time. Be better. Take ownership.

This of course can apply in anything. If you treat your partner poorly and you split up of course it's all them (insert eye roll here). You get another partner who seems to fit you better, but you fall into similar problems with the new partner as you did the old one. It's because of YOU—your attention to detail and your emotional investment.

The bottom line is you get out what you put in!

If you want your circumstances to be different—more money, a better job, or to lose weight— stop looking to others or making excuses why you can't. It starts with you. Take ownership!

As harsh as it may sound, your upbringing or what you have been through doesn't allow you a free pass to give up or to not take responsibility for your actions. No one, not even you is entitled to this kind of thinking or special treatment.

The things that happen at times in life are not always fair, but instead of wallowing in that (and some of us do), we need to practice "radical acceptance" or living life on life's terms. When we stop with the unrealistic expectations or entitlement it paves a path toward living a better, healthier, and more fulfilling life.

When I was going through a situation that cost me dearly, I remember someone said to me, "if anyone can get through this, YOU can."

At the time that got me angry; I didn't want to hear powerful affirmations like that. What I wanted was for people to pity me and feel sorry for me. I wanted them to affirm that wrong had been done to me and to celebrate along with me in my pity party!

At the time I felt they didn't understand what I was going through.

Or did they?

Maybe they saw I was better than what I was letting myself become—hopeless, destitute, and negative.

We have all done it; stayed home watching countless hours of TV to drown out our sorrows to disconnect from the world because it is all too much.

Sometimes it is good to turn off and disconnect. But it's what we do after that. Do we just have the "woe is me" and "life is too hard" attitude? Or do we let the moment pass like traffic; see it, identify it, acknowledge it, and most importantly learn from it?

If we really didn't like the situation we found ourselves in, then we should make sure things like that don't ever happen to us or affect us like that ever again. We must prevent those kinds of patterns.

Do we need to learn what we did to contribute to the outcome and what we can change? Most definitely. We can't change others; that's up to them, even though we try in vain which adds to our own frustration.

We place so much time and effort in trying to "help" them change. Our best efforts are put into them when in reality we are trying help ourselves (and we become distracted from bettering ourselves as well). If we can look at it objectively, we will see that their resistance to our "help" is founded on their moral compass, not ours. So, of course they are not on the same page as us in desiring self-improvement or a more fulfilling life. At least not yet.

Don't bite off more than you can chew

My parents always used this expression. It basically means don't attempt to push beyond the accepted. But who has set what is deemed as acceptable limits?

Roger Bannister was the first human ever to run a mile in 4 minutes. It had never been achieved before him. If he had listened to, "don't bite off more than you can chew," he may never have been the first human to beat the record.

Interestingly enough, once he had run that mile in 4 minutes, suddenly 24 others around the world that same year were able to achieve a 4-minute mile run. It was a pivotal moment in human psychology. It broke through the notion "it can't be done." The new record by Hicham El Guerrouj is 3.43.13.

I have changed this favourite saying of my parents to "Bite off as much as I can and chew like hell!"

Will we be happy when......?

How many of us have heard someone say or even said to ourselves, "I'll finally be happy when __ happens"?

Why do we place so much importance on unobtained material or emotional things in order for us to be happy? Once we get it, we move on to the next thing we "need." Perhaps it's a "want" more than a "need."

Next time you are looking at buying something ask yourself whether you need it, or want it.

Once you get the promotion, the "perfect" partner, or that shiny new toy—will it actually make you happy? Most likely (almost definitely) NO.

What is wrong with appreciating what we have right now? Being present and practicing gratitude, even for the seemingly mundane (your health, the job that puts food on the table, the sun or the rain).

Have we lost the ability to be happy within ourselves so much that we need constant external validation?

Our emotional elevator is running overtime much more so than our parents at the same age.

How so?

Ongoing studies are showing that the emotional elation, sadness, and disappointment we experience on a daily basis from social media could be equivalent to what our parents went through over a 3-6-month period.

So, we have increased the "roller coaster emotional ride" to a daily occurrence.

Two studies involving more than 700 students found that depressive symptoms such as low mood and feelings of worthlessness and hopelessness were linked to the quality of online interactions. Researchers found higher levels of depressive symptoms among those who reported having more negative interactions.

A similar study by the BBC conducted in 2016 involving 1,700 people found a threefold risk of depression and anxiety among people who used the most social media platforms. Reasons for this, they suggested, include cyber-bullying, having a distorted view of other people's lives, and feeling like time spent on social media is a waste.

The rise and fall of some people's emotional elevator depends on how many have liked or commented on their new picture. With this happening on a daily basis, you can see how much overtime a person's emotional elevator is working.

It is no wonder anti-depression and anxiety prescriptions are at an all-time high. In England, the number of prescribed antidepressants over the last 10 years is a massive 108.5% increase on the 31 million antidepressants that pharmacies dispensed in 2006.

In Australia the number of prescribed antidepressants has also doubled in the last decade.

The Centres for Disease Control (CDC) in the U.S. say that since 1988 the prescribed number of antidepressants has risen 400%, and they also claim that two-thirds of people with severe depression aren't on any medication. So, some who need help through medicine to better manage their emotional elevator aren't getting the proper help, and others who might need to look inward for a solution to a malfunctioning emotional elevator are seeking help exclusively through what they believe is a "magic pill." There has to be a balance.

Why aren't many of us treating our emotional elevator properly?

Where is all this stress coming from?

The need or desire to fit in?

The need or desire to be liked?

How can we turn this around?

Is it as simple as getting in and out of our emotional elevator?

Like all things it takes practice. At first changing mood states or levels in our emotional brain is a struggle, but keep at it. The results are worth it. The alternative is perpetual misery—and no one has to or deserves to live like that. Surviving isn't living. It is possible to thrive, even in the face of dire circumstances.

Let's live our lives to the fullest. Start making a list of things you want to do (and not everything has to cost exorbitant amounts of money).

Assess your life and surroundings.

What is it that is making you so unhappy?

Your job? The place you live? Your partner? The state of your bank account?

Take the job situation. What is it you would like to do?

Is there a course you can do after hours to get you qualified for this? Can you find a little time each day to learn about the ins and outs of this kind of work? Can you start meeting people in that line of work or industry? The biggest takeaway is don't settle! There is always a solution. Success is never a straight line. But endless complaining is not part of the recipe for success and neither is a sense of entitlement. It's time to make some changes and improve yourself. Little by little, piece by piece.

You have the control!

"Do what you have to do, until you can do what you want to do."

- Oprah

Let's look at some solutions to some common ruts we find ourselves in.

Question 1. Are you happy with where you are living?

If you are renting, then start looking for a new place. Don't set unrealistic deadlines. Give yourself 3-6 months or longer.

A problem we all seem to have is I want this, and I want it NOW! If I can't have it within the next three days then, "I don't want it anymore. I have lost interest." Surely, we haven't become that fickle, have we?

Make it temporary!

Whatever is making you unhappy where you're living—the broken tap or low water pressure or smell of mould or whatever it is —will not be so hard to deal with because it now has a timeline. This will take the frustration out of where you are living at the moment.

Your mindset will change your outcome and that journey to your new outcome will be less stressful. You will see the "only temporary" attitude will drop the tension away tenfold.

Question 2. Are you 100% happy in your relationship?

Have you sat down and spoken with the other person about the issues at hand?

You need to have an honest sit down with yourself first and be honest about whether you want to work things out with them. How do you feel about them? Can you see a future with them?

If you don't have this conversation with yourself first, then your relationship is doomed to fail because you have no direction or a map of where you want to go. Your desire to fix things for the better has no momentum or direction or "purpose" and you will be easily swayed and led in a direction that may not be optimum for you.

If you are in an unhealthy relationship, then politely show them the door. Life is too short to be wasting on people that are bad for you and your mental health. You only have one life— make it worthwhile!

Question 3. Are you happy with your job?

How can you make some changes? Call on someone to help you. People don't realize there is a struggle unless it is revealed to them. We have discussed this before, but enrol in a course on something you really want to do. Set out a plan—it may take 15 months to complete, but it is moving you forward to something better. Again, it's only temporary!

How long have you been in the job you dislike? A year or 15 months doesn't seem that long.

Question 4. Are you happy with the balance of your bank account?

Sit down and truly look at how you spend your money and what you spend it on.

Do you buy lunch every day at work, plus a coffee or two? That is at least $20 per day, which is $100 a week. That's $400 a month straight away.

Make your lunch, prepare it the night before or in the morning before going to work. It will cost you $20 for ingredients that will probably last longer than a week.

Or take a second job, maybe not indefinitely, but have a timeline in your mind. Set up a separate account just for this goal, an account you can't access that easily. That way your brain can adjust and know that this is only temporary! It's short-term inconvenience for the long-term benefits of raising that bank account. It is important to place time limits on this, otherwise you can become disheartened and it becomes a chore and not a mini-goal. And you can get stuck in a rut because you lack the goal-setting abilities.

Time frames, goals, mindset—it's all only temporary!

Changing our state

How can we change our state? How do we even begin to obtain the skills to get into the elevator and move to a different, more desirable level? Especially if we are in such a depleted state—we don't know which way is up!

Exercise is one method.

I cannot begin to tell you the benefits I have experienced from exercising. Numerous studies have shown the positive effects exercise has on the brain. A good exercise or workout releases healthy hormones and endorphins all throughout our body. Have you ever heard of a runner's high? The formal definition is *a feeling of euphoria that is experienced by some individuals engaged in strenuous running and that is held to be associated with the release of endorphins by the brain.*

Remember when I said, "motion changes emotion"?

Exercising effects our moods and the way we think and in turn the way we handle situations.

In the book *Spark* the authors John J. Ratey MD and Eric Hagerman discuss how they created a "zero" period in school which was a heavy dose of physical exercise before the usual classes started. After implementing "zero" period for an extended period of time, they noticed a huge change not only in the grades of the students, but they seemed happier, more content, and less stressed.

Ratey and Hagerman recall from their own cases where a patient was on antidepressants and through regular exercising were actually weaned off the drug. A pretty bold statement, but all this was done under the watchful care of their doctors. I am not saying by any means that you go for a walk and then throw away your Zoloft!

If you consider this, you would need to work closely with your GP or psychologist and take your time. No need to rush.

Slow to Learn, Slow to Forget

Chapter 8

A Case for Physical Activity

A P.E. instructor at Madison Jr. High in the United States of America, Phil Lawler, is quoted as saying his favourite statistic is that only 3% of adults past the age of 24 stays in shape with exercises and team sports. Yes, 3%!

Do you think if everyone (or even a larger percentage of people) did a little more exercise and had the benefits of the hormones and the endorphins from the runners high we would have as much depression and anger in this world? Do you think people would be better able to tap into their sense of purpose?

We would benefit in a huge way if we spent more mental energy planning our next exercise session instead of ruminating on meaningless things that we assign so much emotion to. We would be able to let those unnecessary emotions pass by like traffic much more easily.

It would be an interesting experiment to see if exercise caused a reduction of "brain chatter" while increasing the individual's overall happiness and sense of purpose. In theory wouldn't the world on a mass scale be happier and less stressful?

Writing this book was not even in my thoughts while I was down and out. It took all my energy to survive day to day with my mask on.

I am actually writing this chapter after a 6am, workout session, a full body cardio workout in 10 degree weather, yet I was sweating head to toe.

Because of my workout my brain feels alive. It is firing, it is inspired, and it is contemplating what else can be done today.

I challenge you. Try it. Get up and go to a gym or a club—not just once or twice, but give it at least three months.

Don't let excuses stop you. *I had a bad knee when I was younger*, or *I have had an operation on my shoulder*. Talk to the trainers and they will help strengthen those areas without letting you damage them. Three months, yes, your muscles will be sore. Yes, it will be hard to walk upstairs—good! That shows growth.

Of course, it is easier to stay comfortable on your couch. But how long will our life be in we sit down on the couch and eat chocolate and fill our bellies with soft drinks?

Start slowly in moderation, then build from there.

I see it all the time, the gung-ho attitude—"I am going to do these five classes and work out seven days this week, and lose ten pounds of fat and gain twenty pounds of muscle." Whoa. Slow down. You may be excited, but that kind of drive is unsustainable in the long run and doesn't last. Plus if you do that much exercise and that many classes in the first two weeks your body will literally go into shock and you'll hardly be able to move. Rest is required, but not too much or you'll fall back into the comfort and ease of the couch.

Moderation is key. Take your time. How long did it take you to become overweight or lethargic? It's going to take a similar amount of time to become fit and active as well.

There is no instant cure, no magic pill. It will take a new, strong mindset. It will require determination, grit, persistence, and control of our emotional elevator. (By the way, I am the worst at moderation. When I find something I really like, I do it like 120% and then some.)

How many of us abide by moderation 24/7 and never deviate? Could I boldly assume not a single one of us? We have all been there, done that. Let me ask you, do we truly learn from things and move on, or do we keep walking the same path, failing and then repeat? Does it all seem a little futile?

I also hear from some people, "Oh, but you are different you are gifted in this area."

No, let me share something with you—I hated running. I forced myself to run because I needed the endurance to obtain my black belt. When I started running, I was running 7.30 minutes per kilometre!

I tried running around my block where I lived, and it wreaked havoc on my knees. Did I give up? It would have been so easy to say, "I tried but my knees just can't take it." I went into solution mode. What can I do that will help achieve my goals with less injury to myself? I found an athletic track where I could go and run that had a rubber compound that was easier to run on. It also happened to be a nice flat surface and it helped with strengthening my knees. Win-win!

By the time I went for my black belt I was running at 4.15 minutes per kilometre. It took 2 years to build up that strength and stamina. So I am not gifted, I just have determination and a never give up attitude.

We are so quick to label, to get in our emotional elevator, and our jealousy or spite spits out excuses or comments and insults to justify our shortcomings or lack of discipline. Funny how people are quick to use the words "natural," or "gifted." On the flip side if all that were true then why do these "gifted" or "naturals" also suffer from depression or the common cold like everyone else? Discipline and achievement are not selective, but a MINDSET!

In an article by Heidi Godman from Harvard Health Publishing she explains that the many reasons for having physical exercise as part of your of weekly routine include reducing the odds of heart disease and diabetes, helping to lose weight, lowering your blood pressure, and also helping prevent depression. Exercising also helps the 'brain fog', aiding in thinking skills and assists the brain to work more efficiently protecting and keeping memories. An added bonus it helps you look and feel better. I am very blessed to know (Hanshi) Tino Ceberano. He is 77 years old and has been practicing and teaching Karate his entire life. I remember interviewing him and his memory was astounding—so precise he could recall dates and the year of whom he had met and trained with. Other studies by Dr. McGinnis (a neurologist at Brigham and Women's Hospital in Boston and an instructor in neurology at Harvard Medical School) suggest that the parts of the brain that control thinking and memory are larger in size in people who exercise regularly opposed to people that don't. In a nutshell, exercise improves mood and sleep and reduces stress and anxiety.

An article from brain HQ goes even further and states that, "From a behavioural perspective, the same antidepressant-like effects associated with 'runner's high' found in humans is associated with a drop in stress hormones." A study from Stockholm showed that the antidepressant effect of running was also associated with more cell growth in the hippocampus, an area of the brain responsible for learning and memory.

The other interesting thing I discovered from my own exercise regime is that my body began to crave better, healthier foods. I remember walking back from karate, craving a V8 drink (a vegetable-based drink). I did not want soft drinks, or lollies, or chocolate, and over time I was mainly eating fruit and meat and better foods that would fuel my body better to help cope and repair my worked muscles, joints, and limbs. It was like my brain was telling me to fuel my body better. I felt my sleep was of greater benefit and I was waking up fresher and more alert. As I got healthier, I felt better within myself, and my self-esteem and desire to do things all became heightened.

I felt the brain fog had lifted. My thoughts were of benefit to me and helping me improve myself. Those who have done a lot of exercises will know what I mean and have felt the same. My mind became more productive and I discovered a real need to become better.

I found little patience for trivial things or even the seemingly mundane like TV shows that only exposed the worst side of human nature. As my body started feeling better and stronger it transformed my mind to be the same. Not "feel" the same but BE the same.

The Ceiling of "Total Exhaustion"

I have experienced an incredible physical and mental transformation through exercising.

Whilst grading through the ranks of the Karate syllabus I discovered a dramatic and astonishing mental and physical change.

I was training, exercising, and working towards each grading. I felt strong and fit and that I knew my required techniques. Each grading always ended the same—you can never be 100% prepared!

Then the night of the grading came around.

The pressure of performance and knowing you would be critiqued brought about a combination of nerves and anxiety. You wanted to stand out and show the instructors you knew your stuff and knew it well, all amounting to being pushed to over your limit.

In our mind, we set a bar we think is high. Some of us want to turn around and go home before we even get halfway to the mark (keep going!). Many of us will get catapulted *way* past our assumed limit. Sometimes when we get past that "limit," we feel the need to throw up or collapse on the floor. That's okay. That's progress.

I know martial arts is not for everyone, but in my experience pushing myself beyond what I thought I was capable of is such a rush and an achievement. It actually leaves me thirsty for more—more endurance, more pushing through my barriers (I have been told by many at that club that I am a freak… I hope that's an endearing term).

That ceiling we thought was "enough" and the limit of our physical and mental toughness we had built towards almost seems laughable after we were pushed further and decided failure wasn't an option.

The grading for karate would last 1.5-2.5 hours, and we were pushed harder and harder, whilst internally wishing that the gruelling physical and mental barrage would end. After the grading the exhaustion that I experienced was actually rewarding, and the former ceiling in my mind became my new base. It was my foundation, my new launching pad to go to the next level. I had to start afresh creating a new comfort zone, a new level of endurance both mentally and physically. It was like the previous levels were burnt away like they never existed. The whole comfort zone and pushing to that so-called "ceiling" was now gone…until the next grading!

What Doesn't Kill You Makes You Stronger!

This is not only true in the exercise world but in life situations as well.

When we get dumped by someone it can be excruciating, devastating, and we can't function properly. If it happens again we are affected, but not as much—we know we have gotten through this before. We become resilient— stronger.

Mortality

It's like when we attend a funeral. At that moment we take stock of our lives and realize our mortality. We decide we should make each day count and be nicer, stress less, want less, and take time out to be a better child, parent, and friend. The sentiment of wanting to change is beautiful, but often a week later back in our routine and life, we go back to who we were before the funeral. The machine, the rat race and the wants and needs take over again.

Even if we tried to attend a funeral every week (a morbid thought) to keep that desire to live life to the fullest we would actually become desensitized to the very impact we were seeking.

Instead of seeking a catalyst to help us live life to the fullest, we can work to make doing so a habit. We can appreciate life and celebrate it every day.

Hug and kiss your loved ones as soon as you see them in the morning. Tell them you cherish them and love them. Sit and have breakfast or any meal with them. Turn your devices off and be there with that person right at that moment. Discuss the day ahead and plan outdoor activities for the weekend. Listen. Appreciate. When doing all of these things take note how much more you're enjoying life and wanting to make it better every day. Work to become more aware of how much more you are connecting with your loved ones and in return feeling loved, valued, and needed.

CHAPTER 9

Making Meaning out of Any Situation in Life

"Things don't have meaning; WE assign meaning to everything!"
- Tony Robbins

I would like to help you change some of your terminologies.

"That person is lucky." To "They have worked hard to get there."

"They are natural or gifted." To "They are determined!"

"I wish I could do that." To "What can I do to achieve that?"

"Why is this happening to me?" To "What have I done to contribute to this outcome and what can I do to change it?"

"This is making me feel..." To "Do I need to expend energy on this?"

"I don't need this right now." To "What do I need to learn from this?"

The Mountain

Previously I mentioned "the mountain". Let's look at this more in depth and how we can "conquer the mountain."

This coincides with gratitude; living in the now and not projecting and relying on that all happiness will come from a future outcome or achievement of goals.

When we take on a new task or an endeavour—a desire, a want, a need—we have our sights set on the achievement of this goal, or "conquering the mountain."

Sometimes it's all we think about, working out ways to achieve or obtain this goal. We start out on what we think is a well mapped out journey. One step in front of the other—determination, endurance, the never give up attitude. We ask ourselves, "how bad do you want this?" Our self-talk is positive and we equip our mind with the right, powerful words we need to energize ourselves. We power on!

We see this "mountain" in front of us and our focus doesn't wain; we courageously set out on the journey.

We endure a few obstacles, pot holes, and they seem to bounce off us in the beginning. Our positive mindset doesn't change.

Then something starts to happen as the journey seems to take longer and the path that was once easy, flat, and straight is now a series of impassable tracks or searing cliff faces that take energy and more brain power to navigate. The mountain in front of us seems the same size as it was in the beginning and all the steps we have taken don't seem to have gotten us anywhere. We become discouraged! *It shouldn't be taking this long. It shouldn't be this hard.*

The "mountain" is looming, self-doubt creeps in, and the emotional elevator descends from the floor of determination to the floor of unhealthy self-talk.

This is when it's time to take a quick breather. Stop looking at the "mountain" for a few seconds. Don't worry, it will still be there when you come back.

Look behind you and take stock of how far you have travelled up this mountain path. Pat yourself on the back and be thankful for traveling as far as you have. You have done this by sheer willpower and determination. When looking back, you may actually be surprised at how far you have travelled.

From there, work to reset your thinking. Pause, breathe, and then breathe again. When you turn back around the "mountain" won't seem so far away or as looming. If everything was easily obtained, then there would be no exceptional people in the world. Everyone would be exactly the same. If it's worth achieving, then it will take some effort.

When in the emotional level of (unhappiness) despair or fatigue, we cannot problem solve. We are all tied up in knots and are close to giving up. But when taking a break to adjust for perspective and rest, we have a new and adjusted mindset which will allow us to see the crevasse or that ledge previously hidden. We can continue on with the same determination we started out at the beginning with and we will complete the task or journey.

We seem to always put ourselves under so much pressure to perform and achieve and it can take away from the actual journey itself. How many quotes do we see that say, it's not so much the destination but the journey along the way?

These steps are responsible for crafting our moral compass, our mindset and our being. This is where we are learning, becoming better at overcoming obstacles and becoming more resilient!

But yet again, it's not enough. Our ego wants and desires more.

Once we climb this initial "mountain" we stay there to bask in our achievement for a short time, then the ego kicks in. We become dissatisfied and restless. We then look over to the next "mountain" to scale and we have to do it ASAP! And on the journey goes, jumping from one achievement to another.

This can be a great way to achieve goals but give yourself credit and take the necessary break for perspective and rest. And recognize your value and self-worth. Bask in the glory of achieving this first "mountain." Enjoy!

And be sure to separate wants from desires and needs. Then, after an appropriate amount of time, see if the desire is still there to climb that next "mountain."

Chapter 10

Work/Life Balance and Setting Boundaries

"After climbing a great hill, one only finds that there are many more hills to climb."

- Nelson Mandela

Working hard towards things is important, but is it possible to be working too hard on the wrong things or going in the wrong direction?

We have to be careful of this, because it is possible that we can be in totally the wrong job that doesn't fit our talents, personality or long-term goals. Are you happy doing what you are doing?

I was in a job that I was fortunate to have. I wasn't an easy employee because I was young and temperamental and at times hot-headed. Some might have said "out of control" at the time.

There were three of us fully qualified employees, an apprentice, and three other part-time helpers. Two of the qualified workers left and two of the part-time helpers also left, so there was an apprentice, one part-time helper and I remaining. The owner expected the diminished number of staff to produce the same amount each week! I have always had an attitude to do what was required (and then some), and I tried my best to maintain the quality and output. I stayed in a misguided attempt to prove I was determined and grateful for the job. But the hours I put in were insane—most of the time as many as 12-14 hours a day. I was constantly getting upper chest infections and becoming sick. I was sacrificing my quality of lifestyle and time working so the owner could maintain and keep his!

I saw no other choice but to quit. My soul knew it wasn't right for me, but my mind was constantly fighting it.

In the next few years I started my own business in a totally different field!

If I had stayed at that job, I probably wouldn't be where I am now, or achieved as much as I have.

In the fifteen years I have been in business for myself, I have only ever taken five sick days. Incredible how we become less sick when we love what we do on a day to day basis, or how much a healthier mindset can affect the body physically.

With that toxic job I once had, I thought I was too important to leave. But a mentor once illustrated that my thinking was flawed. He demonstrated how much I would actually be missed by telling me, "Fill up a bucket with water. Now cup both hands and dip them in the bucket. Pull your hands out. The hole or dint that is left in the water remaining in the bucket is how much impact there will be when you leave."

Exactly. There is no dint or hole. People get replaced and the company keeps going. Just like the world keeps turning, the sun always rises and sets. Quite a sombre thought to have when you pour your heart and soul into a company.

Now let's turn that around. Look at how much impact you can have in your own life or another company or your business with something you love doing. How many lives can you touch and enhance once you have moved on from that soul-destroying place? And I'm not exaggerating, it does destroy your soul; filtering through to your children, friends, and romantic relationships. We can become grumpy, rude, impatient, and a pain to be around. You may start drinking more frequently and in more volume, trying to drown your sorrows or trying to quieten the cries of your soul! All of these negative indicators are signs that the soul or our moral compass is unhappy, destabilized, and it needs to be balanced. Balance is the key to a happy, fulfilling life. We hear this all the time, yet most of us do not know how to go about balancing life.

We should have equal time spent with:

Family / Health / Work / Friends / Yourself / Sleep

It doesn't take much to lose this balance. "I just need to work back a few nights to get on top of things." Those few nights can easily turn into weeks and months. We are creatures of habit. When we allow things to interfere and we lose sight of "US" or the "I" this is when the balance gets out of kilter and makes us miserable. So, make it happen right now. No more putting it off. Do it today!

Another level of our emotional state that we tend to stifle is our creative side. This is an important floor to travel to on our emotional elevator.

When we were younger, we may have played an instrument, played a sport, done gymnastics or engaged in something that fed our creative side. We probably started this at an early age and it almost became part of us. We then got a job and we became too busy and stopped playing our instrument or our sport. Before we know, it years can pass. That creative part of us is dormant and yet we wonder why we become unhappy.

Chapter 11

Eliminating the Drama and Living on Purpose

The Honey Maker

We all have that friend or person we know that has had something or someone do them wrong and every time we see them they tell us about it, like it just happened. It could be two weeks or three months, but whatever the timeframe, they are always strongly emotionally involved with it and the description is explosive. Their agitated energy is almost too difficult to be around. We try hard not to judge them, or roll our eyes, or find an excuse to walk away.

Are you ever "that person?" That annoying friend who ruminates on things, keeping things alive and giving up space in your brain about someone or something (that in the end is meaningless) that has done you wrong?

Are you someone who has a "bee in your bonnet?" Let me describe what I call the "honey maker." This is where the person is ruminating and holding onto a situation so tightly their knuckles are white, their teeth have sunken in, and their jaw is clenched! The bee is so busy, it is making honey! It's like they are waiting to catch up with people so they can tell them of all the wrong that has been done to them. For what? Sympathy? To feel supported, cared for, important?

We have discussed the very same thing in this book—keeping situations alive.

We can't do anything about it when we are out at a dinner or at the movies or at a friend's place. Let the bee out! The longer we let the bee spin and live in our "bonnet" the more honey is created. Stop the bee from making its honey! Stop keeping the situation alive.

Let it go and get in your elevator and move to a different level. Be thankful, be happy, be mindful. Do whatever you need to do to move past the situation. This will take a lot of practice and time. The more often you let the bee out, the less time the bee or its sting will have a presence in your life. The big payoff is being happier and less stressed.

Don't be that friend that everyone wants to avoid because you're too busy making honey!

Bees sting. They hurt like hell and some of us are allergic to them, but bees die after they have stung. Try and do the same when you have a difficult situation in your life—feel the sting, have the discomfort, nurture the sting, treat the wound, and then let it heal and move on. Let the bee die! Clear your "bonnet!"

Do we have an obligation?

Why should I bother attempting to change my emotional state and guide my moral compass if everyone else doesn't? Why should I put myself through the self-analysis if others can't be bothered doing the same?

These questions are commonly asked and felt after going through an adjusmtent period.

1. Are you 100% happy with how things were before?
2. Are you tired of getting the same results?
3. Are you trying to reduce stress in your life?
4. Are you seeking happiness?

Final question—Do you live your life according to what others expect?

If the answer to all the above except question 4 is "no," then yes, you have an obligation to yourself to become better, to evolve with intention.

It's not up to you to change others! That is up to them. Everyone has a different journey to their enlightenment or awakening. It is not your task to enforce that on others. You can lead by example, but not demand others follow your lead.

It is up to you to change and improve yourself. You have bought this book to do just that, not to read it and tell everyone else what to do.

It has taken me many years to identify and analyse reoccurring circumstances and to really want to make a change. Becoming a parent was a huge step. Failed relationships also contributed. Having nice things seemed important to me, but the machine overtook me. I found I was sacrificing my quality of life just to keep what I had—missing out on valuable time in my boys' growing and learning years. I wasn't present enough, always looking to the next thing on the horizon. I was allowing and even choosing (taking ownership here) to be distracted and lose sight of what was important—health, happiness, and an enriched life.

So, if that is not obligation enough, I am not sure what is. We all have different motivations.

Just like someone else's bad mood can affect us if we allow it to, our mood can influence others' moods as well. As you gain more control of your emotions and achieve better outcomes for yourself, this, in turn, will be infectious in others. These seemingly small moments will add up and make this world a tad more civilized and less stressful.

Remember it's not about what others do to you. It is how you let their actions affect you—and which level you ALLOW your elevator to travel to.

Control your elevator, adjust your moral compass and start enjoying smoother sailing and less stress. You CAN be better!

There are times when the personality types of the people we involve ourselves with are narcissistic, or just plain obstinate, and no matter what we do it has little to no effect. It is best to distance yourself from those types of people.

Give Yourself Purpose

It always amazes me how our posture and how we physically feel can affect our mindset, and how our mindset can control our body.

The mind will give up before the body will!

Here is something we can all identify with. You are at work and you are tired of the constant, boring, uninteresting grind—the same day in, day out. At one point it feels like 30 minutes have passed by. You check the clock and it has only been 3 minutes.

You yawn and struggle to do the simplest of things. To top it off you become so distracted and mentally numb you become clumsy; knocking over your drink or deleting the wrong email or walking into walls. You even fall asleep while on the toilet. All day your thoughts are cloudy and you find it hard to pay attention.

That night you have something you really want to do—exercise, dance class, or maybe painting a room in your house. As soon as you get wherever it is you want to be after work, you have a tremendous burst of vigour and energy. You are almost jumping out of your skin with the excess energy. You have almost reached a euphoric state.

You can't wipe the smile off your face, yet not more than a few minutes earlier you could hardly keep your eyes open. Your brain had switched off and you were exhausted.

What happened?

It was a shift in mindset. You took a trip in your emotional elevator and became that emotion; excited, happy, and ready to achieve your end result. That alone changed your physiology.

By changing your emotional state, your mindset, you have physically changed the way your body feels! And when your body feels good it helps your mind feel the same, and so the cycle goes.

What can we learn from this mind-altering physiological change?

If we give ourselves a purpose, a task, something to achieve; we will not get bogged down in the mundane aspects of life. We will have tremendous mental and physical benefits.

It's kind of like a mini-mountain scenario mentioned earlier. Set a task for yourself or set a goal, something to raise your sights toward.

It's amazing how energized we can feel by having a purpose.

It also distracts our brain from dwelling on the negative and helps us to stop wasting time ruminating over silly little things that when given too much power and energy become huge boulders in front of us. An intentional task or goal will help prevent us from becoming unhappy, miserable, depressed, and exhausted!

So next time you are feeling uninspired and drained, ask "why?"

Set a task. Start with small ones. Maybe a small household chore like a carwash. Maybe it's cleaning off the bikes and going for a ride. Perhaps it's getting the family together and trying that new restaurant you have been thinking about.

Whatever you choose to do, make it something you've never done or haven't done in a while.

The other benefit from this is you will have more things to discuss with other people—better conversations, sharing positive things instead of being "that" guy that hasn't gotten over the situation and tells the same story over and over again (insert eye roll).

Chapter 12

The Seed

Our mind, thoughts, and pre-motivated projections can be super destructive.

What's a pre-motivated projection? It's just a fancy term for an assumption.

From our moral compass, we try and predict the future from the scenario presented to us, based on a past blueprint that we have experienced from other situations in our life.

We question if every outcome we experience has the same motivation behind it. We might ask: *what's the common denominator here,* or *does everyone have the same motivation—to hurt me, rip me off, or step on me to better their own position?*

If you dwell on negatives you will attract negative outcomes.

Try to rewire and create a new neural pathway in your brain to STOP that kind of mindset. Find a way to get in your elevator, change levels, change your state, think differently and look at each situation from a different perspective. Take ownership of your part in the situation— which is about it as far as predetermined outcomes go.

The common denominator is always you. It is your thinking and your projection that constantly leads you to a similar outcome.

In essence you almost create the same outcome just from your (negative) thoughts!

People treat you the way you teach them to treat you!

This analogy isn't that dissimilar to the old Cherokee two wolf story.

An old Cherokee is teaching his young grandson some valuable life lessons

He sits and says to his grandson, "Inside of me and everyone including you there is a constant fight between two wolves. One is evil, spiteful and angry, full of lies and deception. The other is good. He has love, joy, compassion and is humble."

The grandson was worried and took his time, but he asked his wise grandfather, "I don't understand, which wolf will win?"

The old Cherokee replied, "Simple, my grandson. The one you feed."

Our brain, or more so our thoughts, try to justify every situation with only a tiny bit of information. Our thoughts always tend to be suspicious that everyone is conniving to do us wrong. We create what we believe is the motivation behind the situation, because we believe we have it sorted and know it all! A veritable Sherlock Holmes in our own mind.

Sometimes we can create a whole floor plan from a simple sentence that we latch on to, making it bigger than what it really is.

We may even go as far as asking questions, and when the answer doesn't fit in with what we've deduced, we ask more questions and manipulate them to entrap the person, so it fits in with our thinking.

This is so far removed from the truth or the facts. Have you actually asked the person the meaning behind their action or statement?

Perhaps it's like the following metaphor: You have a seed. You believe that if you plant this seed and water it and feed it, a particular plant will grow from it. It will sprout leaves and grow towards the sun. However, will a chicken or milk or anything else sprout from the seed—even if you believe it or tell yourself a million times that it will? No!

You are stacking the outcome to serve your own belief system.

Throw away the seed, start afresh, and have a clear field. Let the unbiased answers to your questions plough the field and let the fruit yield on its own. Do not pre-plant seeds and collect the seeds from the questions answered before they have time to grow.

You have stacked the field to suit your own beliefs, or perhaps even your own ego and pride.

Here is a simple little emotional mindset check-in for you to implement.

Ask yourself what do I know of this situation? What are the actual facts?

As soon as you start making assumptions instead of taking in facts, stop and throw away the preconceived seed. Let the field be ploughed with facts. Start fresh. Do not assume! And let the field develop in front of you. Leave your Sherlock Holmes hat at home!

Pro Tip: The only reason this would not be applicable is if you have video evidence or a recording that contradicts the answers you are receiving from the person involved. Unfortunately, it may take a lot of planning and slight paranoia to get this information—not to mention the agonizing hours of worry!

Let's take all of this a step further.

Get into your elevator and travel up to the empathy level.

When a person charges you with something untrue, to them it may certainly feel that way.

Be empathetic and remove the emotion and the pride and look at it from their side.

You can respond with:

- I can understand how you see it that way.
- I can understand how you might feel that way.

Be careful, because if this is just lip service you will get caught. If you want to help those around you cause and receive less stress, be sincere!

They have their own blueprint, their own feelings, and their own moral compass. It is our job to recognize this and take ownership. Pop your hand up, admit fault, and sincerely apologize.

This is the beginning of healing and sorting through situations in the shortest amount of time possible without all the baggage and previous blueprints that serve our own pre-conceived ideas.

Start living better—become better time managers doing things that are good for you and others. Live life, enjoy your time, and do not be an avoider!

Do not waste your life fighting with people, stressing, worrying or ruminating.

Control which level your emotional elevator lands on.

Now, this is a tough mindset to break away from. As we learn and develop we assume that everyone around us is learning at the same rate as us. We expect all of those around us are in the same classroom. We expect everyone else to share our moral compass. Wrong!

This is the "Planet Me" scenario—I'm the centre of the universe and everyone orbits me and thinks the way I think!

Some of us expect all the people around us to understand us and be at our beck and call whenever we need them. We might even treat people poorly if we feel they aren't there for us. We demand their attention.

This is you acting like a planet, and you think of your friends and family as satellites that should be in your orbit.

You can probably identify people you know that have the Planet Me syndrome.

You know the people that only call you up when they have a problem because you listen and make them feel good? That's a Planet Me person.

The first and most paramount thing we need to understand: no one is on the same journey as we are.

Remember our moral compass? This is what defines us.

No two people will have exactly the same moral compass—maybe similar, but we will still have differing points and triggers.

The biggest mistake we can make is expecting our partners and family and friends to be learning at the same rate we are.

Yes, it will be frustrating. Yes it will be as clear as a blue sky to you how or which way one should act or react to a situation—but your "clarity" is not their clarity.

The more you try and force someone to take ownership or see things your way, the further you push them away and alienate them and the longer and more heated the discussion becomes.

Patience is required. One of my all-time favourite dad jokes is "If I wanted patience I'd become a doctor," (insert laughter and applause).

We need to be a good educator, not pompous and arrogant with our knowledge.

We need to gently help the other person see a different way of looking at the situation or changing their emotional state. This is how you get someone to sheepishly pop up their hand and say, "yep I am at fault here." But they need to be able to do that on their own—not to be told or even berated to do so. The realization that they need to take ownership will happen on their time, not yours. If they do it because they were told to it now becomes a controlled situation and resentment can creep in—and you are bordering on being a control freak, which is no good for anyone. When they choose to do it, the impact is far greater and longer lasting.

Your focus needs to be on YOU taking ownership instead of a *quid pro quo* deal—I will if you will.

If the other person is berating you and you've taken ownership try something like, "Hey, can you see I have popped up my hand and taken ownership," or, "I am sorry I let my pride and ego cloud my reaction. I have fixed that now. Please let me apologize."

And leave it there! Don't then try to tell them all of their faults and how they've harmed you.

When diffusing a situation by taking ownership and changing your emotional state, you may be surprised at what happens next.

Because the tension has subsided and there is no yelling, that person may take a step back, which allows their emotional elevator to get out of the red warning stage. Their elevator will travel to a different level by its own accord and you may find their rationale and apologies start to flow. But do not place any expectations on this—be responsible for yourself.

Those that have no desire to resolve the situation may reply with, "You should apologize. It was all your fault and not mine." For them it's about winning, not resolving and forging forward together stronger or amicably. If you have people like that in your life distance yourself from them and have as little as you can with them. They have a fixed mindset and will exhaust you and drag you down.

You don't deserve that kind of constant negativity in your life. We are on a quest to be happier and reach new heights with our personal development. Their actions and reactions say more about them than you.

Dealing with someone who is not aware or interested in taking ownership or changing or controlling their mindset is actually good practice for us, to let their emotions wash over us. Don't ignore them, but identify how much they are letting the situation affect them. Instil great emotional restraint within and keep your own elevator where you want it. Don't let their harsh words or yelling affect your mindset or where your elevator is. Remember, you are in control! It's great practice to solidify your emotional intelligence.

Please don't feel bad if you take ownership and they don't reciprocate. Know in your soul that you have done well in your self-development to identify their emotions and yours, effectively reducing your own stress and anxiety.

From there we need to then let it go. Do not dwell on why they didn't take ownership.

Acknowledge that you have done everything you can and be hopeful that one day they may be enlightened and start to control their mindset and state and take ownership. But it is not your responsibility to help and convert everyone. They need to want to change, sense it, feel it, and then desire it before we can help them.

If you feel someone would benefit from seeing a psychologist and you tell them, it's no surprise they might resist or become offended. It has to be their conscious decision. See how much our emotions govern our actions!

You may get the opportunity one day to help impart to them what you have learned if they come to you in despair.

We are all traveling on a journey at different stages and momentum. We so desperately want to run back and hurry people along to "catch up. Remember this very important fact—it is your journey, not anyone else's. You don't need permission or to have a crew of supporters cheering you on. You are resilient and strong enough to walk the journey.

I have been in the situation where I am learning all this, gaining better control and almost pushing or forcing it on others. I want to share my light bulb moment with everyone—like the Tasmanian Devil from the Looney Tunes cartoon whizzing at 100 miles an hour screaming, "You have to learn what I've learned and do what I'm doing NOW!"

It has taken me so long to reach this part of my journey and it's ridiculous of me to expect everyone else to appreciate where my journey has brought me. It's my compass.

In the beginning, I would let a person's rejections stifle my own energy and passion. I would pull back and quieten myself down and stop working toward my own personal development.

You and I, we are on our own journey of self-improvement. It is not a team effort.

This could almost sound selfish and arrogant—but in the end, each of us is responsible for ourselves and no one else. We need to again take ownership of our actions, our moods, and how we affect others around us.

When we are the best versions of ourselves, we are better for those around us. We will be the person that others enjoy and want to be around because we have a positive energy emanating from us.

Most of all we will be happier within ourselves that we have achieved all we set out to achieve. No one can hold us back; only we can hold ourselves back.

If you haven't achieved what you have set out to do, maybe you have the wrong people around you, or maybe you are not asking the right questions.

Stay true to your course, never settle, don't let a small bump in the road give you permission to throw your hands in the air and give up.

As soon as we start blaming others for our own failings, it is then that we have lost our way!

It is your emotional elevator and you are in control of it. Others may try and push your buttons, but ultimately, it is up to you which floor you let your emotional elevator land on.

Take ownership, stop blaming others, be humble and be better.

There is only one you. Make it the best it can be!

Chapter 13

Final Thoughts

The back story

Have you ever created a scenario in your mind and wanted to share something with someone and have everything perfect, yet when the occasion arises you feel let down? You may even be annoyed or angry because things didn't go the way you had hoped or imagined.

Quite often we build up a movie or engage in fake role play in our mind way before we even meet up with the person. This is similar to the argument scenario, but on the other spectrum.

The disappointment comes from the outcome being less than you desired. Basically, it didn't go the way you wanted. Our brains are so programmed from movies we believe if we imagine and see the outcome it will follow.

But we can't control the other person one bit. We have no idea what they have endured in that day or how well they have slept or how well they are feeling.

We expect them to have lived in our head and seen the same vision we have or, to be on the same page—to play the part we have set out for them.

How do you expect them to know what is going on in your head? How can you expect them to play their part so you can feel good and have your movie moment and be fulfilled?

Instead of planning out an unrealistic scenario, you could be vulnerable. Say *I have this vision I want to play out*, or *I am going to do this*, or *I love you so much*, or *I am coming over to take you out* or *I need this from you*. It takes the spontaneity out of it, but it kills the disappointment of things backfiring. Better yet, your little inner child has no room to step in and stomp around in a tantrum when you don't get your way.

It is not fair to expect anyone to understand or share something with you if you do not give them the back story.

It may originate from the utmost love you feel towards someone and how much you cherish them, and so you want to celebrate that with them. But next time try explaining this to them—don't try to write a script in advance. Be flexible. Allow the other person to have their moment within your moment so it is a shared experience and both parties can reflect on it.

****

My pursuit of understanding the emotions and how they affect our actions and reactions has come from my young adulthood. Back them I had no filter and let my emotions dictate my actions. I was emotionally out of control and in turn it was how others saw me and defined me as a person.

I did not like the way I was perceived, and my soul cried out telling me I was better than that. I had to learn, be better, achieve more, and do it in the most congruent way!

I had to take ownership. I started reading books not dissimilar to this to help forge my path to be better, become more, and experience a fulfilling life!

If I can reshape my moral compass, I am sure you can as well. It will depend on your desire and commitment to make the changes necessary.

You will notice that in my emotional elevator metaphor, I refer to moving downwards for the negative emotions of anger, fear, despair, and jealousy. These are the emotions that weigh us down, the negatives that make us drag our feet and stunt us moving forward and living a fulfilled and stress-free life. The higher levels I feel are lighter, brighter, closer to the sky, the sun and the stars, and make us weightless, the way astronauts float through space—effortless and fun. This is how I want life to be. Why is it when we are looking for hope and changes in our situation we look up? It gives us hope and the freedom to fly and makes our horizons limitless! With your newfound control of your emotional elevator you will be able to achieve more, have more energy and create a happier life for yourself and the people around you.

I hope this book has helped you in your pursuit of happiness and a less stressful life. Being in a happier, more positive state will free up your mind and will kickstart your creative mind into achieving much more. You will have a sense of fulfilment because of everything you're accomplishing. Your head will hit your pillow each night with the satisfaction of doing and having the right amount of energy to jam pack your day with so much!

You will hopefully start to feel that it is not about time management as much as it is an energy management—making YOU happier!

I definitely don't have it all sorted out and I do have bad days and don't always apply what I am writing about. But I'm human! Our brains are emotionally wired, and sometimes make automatic decisions and choices without any conscious thought. It just reacts. Sometimes it's mostly for the good (fear helps us keep safe), but other times it can be detrimental to our wellbeing and others around us.

One of the biggest realizations most people need to make is we are all hypocrites, and I don't say that in a judgmental way. If we can identify that and take ownership, it will help resolve a whole series of events.

A lot of the time we say things and then do the complete opposite, or our expectations of others are unrealistic because we change what we say and do.

It doesn't take much to stick your hand up, to be accountable and take ownership. It is actually quite humbling and allows you to achieve tremendous mental growth.

Change your state by being aware of how the assigned emotion will cause you to act or react. Then reverse-engineer your outcome and use your elevator to change your mood—it will change your outcome!

Remember we are human *beings* not, human *doings*.

We are all too busy just doing things, not being present, or aiming to be better than yesterday.

Be in the moment, be patient, be considerate, be understanding, be happier.

Be on the emotional level that you desire.

About The Author

Experiencing a major setback a few years ago, Stuart discovered that life doesn't always go as planned. As he was temporarily unable to change his course at the time, he in turn headed for the road of self-destruction and isolation. Forced to take a really good, hard look at himself, he slowly reconstructed from the ground up. Stuart poured himself into reading and learning many a different way to overcome the hurdles put before him. He discovered that part of who he is and who he was meant to be was to help others feel good about themselves - even if that meant cracking a corny dad joke to get a smile. Stuart studies life, philosophy, martial arts, and is on a quest to have a better experience and quality of living. Ultimately, his ideal goal in life is to have the world a more harmonious place than where it stands currently. Through Stuart's lived experience and what he has learned during his journey up until this point has been penned in this book with the hope of helping you understand your own *emotional elevator.*

Printed in the United States
By Bookmasters